Eat Great, Lose Weight, Feel Healthy

THE QUINTESSENTIAL

Quinoa Cookbook

WENDY POLISI

SKYHORSE PUBLISHING

Skyhorse Publishing books may be purchased in bulk at special discounts for sales promotion, corporate gifts, fund-raising, or educational purposes. Special editions can also be created to specifications. For details, contact the Special Sales Department, Skyhorse Publishing, 307 West 36th Street, 11th Floor, New York, NY 10018 or info@skyhorsepublishing.com.

Skyhorse® and Skyhorse Publishing® are registered trademarks of Skyhorse Publishing, Inc.®, a Delaware corporation.

Visit our website at www.skyhorsepublishing.com.

10 9 8 7 6 5 4 3 2 1

Library of Congress Cataloging-in-Publication Data is available on file.

ISBN: 978-1-61608-535-3

Printed in China

A culinary pleasure cruise through a South American staple

Table *of* Contents

Entrees & Sides

Quinoa Pasta, Polenta & Pizza

INTRODUCTION

One of the greatest discoveries I've made is that just because food is healthy doesn't mean that it has to taste terrible.

Growing up in the '70s and '80s, I was taught that healthy food tasted bad. When you went on a diet, you lived on celery sticks, carrots and grapefruit and tried not to complain too loudly. Most of us knew so little about nutrition back then, and it never once occurred to me that whole fresh foods could also taste delicious!

I've always been an all-or-nothing kind of person, and it has taken me some time to realize that there is a happy medium. While most of the recipes you will find in this book are undeniably healthy, there are also a few indulgences for those times when you feel like you need something a little special or you are going to go off the reservation! Eating perfectly all the time just isn't a reality for most of us, but we can still nourish our bodies in the process of feeding our souls.

An amazing thing I've discovered is how well quinoa blends into dishes. It can add substance and nutrition without standing out, making it perfect to make indulgent dishes a bit healthier.

I've tried to give alternatives and variations when I can, but I must confess that gluten-free eating is not my strong point. Although I am trying to learn, if you are someone who must follow a gluten-free diet, please make sure that you consult with your health professionals and don't take my word that something is gluten-free. It is always important to read labels and take responsibility for your health.

Let's take a look at the different types of quinoa you will see used in this book.

Quinoa Seeds

When people talk about quinoa, most of the time what they are referring to is quinoa seeds. I don't know about you, but I was actually very surprised when I learned that there are actually 1800 varieties of quinoa. Some are as tiny as a grain of sand, but most of what we see commercially is closer to the size of a sesame seed. Although quinoa can be brown, yellow or orange, most often you will find white, red and black.

Recipes are written for white quinoa, although red and black will work just fine in any recipe. The darker quinoas have a slightly firmer texture and do not absorb water as well. For this reason, you should use about 15% less liquid or plan on draining the quinoa when you are done cooking. You may also cook it a bit longer. Just be careful not to overcook because overcooked quinoa resembles glue and also loses its flavor.

Quinoa Flakes

Quinoa flakes are a bit like oatmeal and can be used in place of oatmeal in most cases. They are good in baking, added to smoothies and as baby food. In fact, it is my understanding that there is a baby food line in the works using quinoa flakes as its base!

Quinoa Flour

Quinoa flour is ground from quinoa seeds. If you've never tried quinoa flour, don't let the smell put you off. It smells like a cross between sneakers and dirt—a definite "earthy" flavor. While it seems a bit strong, when you bake with it, the flavor becomes quite nutty, almost resembling nut butter.

Quinoa Pasta

Quinoa pasta is a real delight! While my family does not care for the taste of whole wheat pastas, we all enjoy quinoa pasta. It is most often gluten-free, making it an excellent alternative for those following a gluten-free diet. One thing to keep in mind when cooking quinoa pasta—while the package rightfully warns against overcooking, you should also be very careful not to undercook. Test a piece to make sure it is done before you remove it. More than once I've ended up with a batch of hard pasta.

Quinoa Polenta

You can purchase quinoa polenta in long tubes and use it just like any other polenta. In fact, if you want to try the polenta recipes in this book but can't find quinoa polenta, feel free to substitute the polenta of your choice.

Because some of the recipes in this book call for cooked quinoa, I'm including basic cooking instructions. One thing to keep in mind is that the many varieties of quinoa, combined with the fact that everyone's stove is a bit different, means that cooking quinoa perfectly can take a bit of tweaking. It is smart to use visual cues to let you know the quinoa is done. As soon as the tail of the germ starts to pop out, test the quinoa to see if it is done. Always remember that the quinoa will continue to cook a bit as you let it sit off the stove covered.

How to Cook Quinoa

Step One: Always Rinse Your Quinoa!

If you are working with unrinsed quinoa, you want to start off by soaking your quinoa. You can soak for an hour or more without a negative impact, but 15 minutes will do the trick. (Some health experts actually recommend soaking for 8 hours, but if you do soak for this long keep in mind that it will not take as long to cook.) After soaking, rinse for 2 or 3 minutes in a fine metal strainer. If you do not have a colander that is fine enough, you can line your regular colander with cheesecloth to get the job done. If you are using pre-rinsed quinoa you can skip this step.

Step Two:

Add 1 part quinoa to 1 1/4 parts liquid. As always, choose the liquid that best suits the dish you are making. Depending on what you are adding to the quinoa as it cooks, you may or may not use a bit more liquid. Bring to a simmer (NOT A BOIL) and then reduce to low. Cover and cook for between 30 and 35 minutes. Remove from heat and let sit covered for an additional 5 minutes.

Alternative Cooking Methods

How to Cook Quinoa in a Rice Cooker

Cooking quinoa in a rice cooker is very simple, but you should be prepared for a bit of tweaking. You will want to use your white rice setting, but make sure that you do not skip rinsing. Use twice as much liquid as quinoa, and to prevent sticking you may want to put a tablespoon of olive oil on the bottom of your cooker. Pay attention to the time that it cooks, so that you can make adjustments next time. Some models tend to slightly overcook the quinoa, but by being aware you can make adjustments.

How to Cook Quinoa when You are Short on Time

Quinoa can actually be prepared in just 20 minutes, and the sacrifice of texture is worth it when you are short on time. To do this, you will need twice as much liquid as you have quinoa. Bring the liquid and quinoa to a boil, and then reduce to medium low. Cover and simmer for 15 minutes. Remove from heat and allow to sit covered for 5 minutes.

A Few Things to Remember

One thing to keep in mind is that 1 cup of quinoa will yield 3 cups of cooked quinoa. Quinoa stores in the refrigerator for up to a week, so it's a good idea to go ahead and cook a couple of cups on the weekend so that you have it on hand for recipes. It's great as a simple breakfast with fruit and nuts or added to a salad.

P eople who try quinoa for the first time often do so because they have been told that it is a nutritious food that they should be including in their diets. What's the big deal? Why is it called a "super food" or a "power food"? Let's take a closer look into quinoa nutrition.

The Perfect Protein

Most people know that quinoa is rich in protein, but what is important to understand when you are talking about quinoa is that it isn't the quantity of protein that is important. (Although 8 grams of protein per serving for a plant based food is pretty strong.) There are plenty of vegetarian foods that are rich in protein. Take beans, for example. Both wheat and oats have almost as much protein as quinoa, but barley, corn and rice have less than half of the protein content.

Quinoa's nutritional significance is more about the quality of the protein than the quantity.

The reason that quinoa is so important is because it is a perfect protein—often called "complete". It contains all 9 of the amino acids that we need for health. This is especially important to vegetarians and vegans, who in the past were encouraged to be obsessed with the idea of combining foods to meet their nutritional needs. (A practice we now know is not necessary.)

According to the Food and Agriculture Organization of the UN, the protein content of quinoa is equivalent in quality to that found in dehydrated whole milk. Of course, quinoa doesn't have all the fat that whole milk does!

One reason that quinoa has gained so much attention is that it is particularly rich in lysine. This essential amino acid is required for cellular repair and also plays other important roles in the body, such as aiding in the absorption of calcium and helping collagen develop. Do you suffer from cold sores? If so, you want to pay careful attention to your lysine intake because new evidence suggests that lysine may help prevent outbreaks.

More than Just Protein

The health benefits of quinoa go way beyond just the exceptional protein content. It is rich in enzymes, phytonutrients, antioxidants, fiber, vitamins and minerals. When you compare quinoa to corn, wheat or barley, it is higher in calcium, manganese, phosphorous, zinc, potassium, copper, magnesium and iron. Here a few other things to know about quinoa nutrition.

- Phytonutrients and antioxidants are believed to help stabilize blood sugar levels
- Quinoa is especially rich in manganese, which is known to activate enzymes for the metabolism of cholesterol and carbohydrates. It is also a great antioxidant that can help your body eliminate toxins.
- It is a good source of magnesium, which helps to relax blood vessels and muscles, which may be helpful for those with both migraines and high blood pressure.
- The fiber content of quinoa can help to tone your colon and is believed to work as a pre-biotic, feeding microflora to your intestines.
- Most grain foods are very acidic, which is believed to cause health issues. (This is why we hear so much about following an alkaline diet.) Quinoa is considered neutral, and is a good alternative for those who are concerned about a candida yeast overgrowth. Grains feed yeast and in some individuals can cause a systemic fungal infection with numerous health implications.

A Look at Quinoa as Compared to Other Grains (% dry weight)

Grain	Water	Protein	Fat	Carbohydrate	Fiber	Ash
Barley	11.1	8.2	1.0	78.8	.5	.9
Buckwheat	11.0	11.7	2.4	72.9	9.9	2.0
Corn	72.7	3.5	1.0	22.1	.7	.7
Millet	11.8	9.9	2.9	72.9	3.2	2.5
Oats	12.5	13.0	5.4	66.1	10.6	3.0
Quinoa	11.4	16.2	6.9	63.9	3.5	3.3
Rice	12.0	7.5	1.9	77.4	.9	1.2
Rye	11.0	9.4	1.0	77.9	.4	.7
Wheat	13.0	14.0	2.2	69.1	2.3	1.7

Source: Wood, R.T. "Tale of a food survivor: Quinoa," *East West Journal*, April 1985, pp 64–68.

Here is a complete breakdown of the nutritional value of one cup of cooked quinoa:

Nutrient	Units	1.00 X 1 cup 185g
Proximates		
Water	g	132.48
Energy	kcal	222
Energy	kJ	931
Protein	g	8.14
Total lipid (fat)	g	3.55
Ash	g	1.41
Carbohydrate, by difference	g	39.41
Fiber, total dietary	g	5.2
Starch	g	32.62
Minerals		
Calcium, Ca	mg	31
Iron, Fe	mg	2.76
Magnesium, Mg	mg	118
Phosphorus, P	mg	281
Potassium, K	mg	318
Sodium, Na	mg	13
Zinc, Zn	mg	2.02
Copper, Cu	mg	0.355
Manganese, Mn	mg	1.167
Selenium, Se	mcg	5.2
Vitamins		
Vitamin C, total ascorbic acid	mg	0.0
Thiamin	mg	0.198
Riboflavin	mg	0.204
Niacin	mg	0.762
Vitamin B-6	mg	0.228
Folate, total	mcg	78
Folic acid	mcg	0
Folate, food	mcg	78
Folate, DFE	mcg_ DFE	78

Nutrient	Units	1.00 X 1 cup 185g
Vitamins		
Vitamin B-12	mcg	0.00
Vitamin A, RAE	mcg_ RAE	0
Retinol	mcg	0
Vitamin A, IU	IU	9
Vitamin E (alpha-tocopherol)	mg	1.17
Tocopherol, beta	mg	0.06
Tocopherol, gamma	mg	2.20
Tocopherol, delta	mg	0.20
Lipids		
Cholesterol	mg	0
Amino acids		
Tryptophan	g	0.096
Threonine	g	0.242
Isoleucine	g	0.290
Leucine	g	0.483
Lysine	g	0.442
Methionine	g	0.178
Cystine	g	0.117
Phenylalanine	g	0.342
Tyrosine	g	0.154
Valine	g	0.342
Arginine	g	0.629
Histidine	g	0.235
Alanine	g	0.339
Aspartic acid	g	0.653
Glutamic acid	g	1.073
Glycine	g	0.400
Proline	g	0.444
Serine	g	0.326

USDA National Nutrient Database for Standard Reference, Release 23 (2010)
Source: http://www.nal.usda.gov/fnic/foodcomp/cgi-bin/list_nut_edit.pl

Quinoa Breakfast Recipes

This is simple to make, but oh so delicious! I like to use Fage Greek yogurt because it is extremely thick and creamy, but any brand will do! If hot sauce is a little much for you feel free to leave it off. I consider a salad with garlic balsamic vinaigrette appropriate for breakfast, so consider the source and decide what works for you.

Chili Rellenos Breakfast Casserole

DIRECTIONS:

1. Preheat oven to 350 degrees. In a large bowl, beat together eggs and egg whites.

2. In a separate bowl, whisk together yogurt and milk until well combined. Add to eggs.

3. Stir in 1 cup of cheese, green chilies, quinoa, salt, pepper and hot sauce to taste. Place in prepared pan.

4. Top with remaining ½ cup of cheese and bake for 30 minutes.

4 eggs

8 eggs whites (or 4 whole eggs)

½ cup Greek yogurt (nonfat)

½ cup low-fat milk

Hot sauce, to taste

1½ cups cheese

4 oz chopped green chilies

1 cup cooked quinoa

Make it Cleaner: Use all egg whites and low-fat cheese.

Make it Vegan: In the bowl of a blender mix together 12 oz of silken tofu and 6 oz of almond milk. Add in ¼ cup nutritional yeast if desired. Use vegan cheese and proceed with the dish.

Make it Gluten-Free: Make sure the hot sauce that you choose is gluten-free and also be sure to read the label on the green chilies. Most are gluten-free, but be sure to check.

6 servings
Calories 291 Total Fat 14.2g Saturated Fat 7.2g Trans Fat 0.0g Cholesterol 156mg 52% Sodium 326mg Total Carbohydrates 21.6g Dietary Fiber 6.0g Sugars 10.2g

A reader asked me to come up with a breakfast casserole that would fit into her very small oven. This recipe is easily scalable for holidays or any time you are serving more than four!

Easy Breakfast Casserole

6 eggs

½ cup milk

½ cup low-fat cottage cheese

1 cup cheddar cheese, divided

1 cup cooked quinoa

¼ tsp crushed red pepper

½ tsp mineral sea salt

½ tsp ground black pepper

½ tsp onion powder

½ tsp Italian seasoning

DIRECTIONS:

1. Preheat oven to 350 degrees. Prepare a medium baking dish with olive oil spray.

2. In a medium bowl, whisk eggs. Add in milk and beat until combined. Stir in red pepper, sea salt, black pepper, onion powder and Italian seasoning. Add cottage cheese, quinoa, and half of cheddar cheese. Pour into baking dish and top with remaining cheese.

3. Bake for 30 minutes. If desired, brown top by placing under broiler for 2 or 3 minutes.

Make it Cleaner: Use 3 eggs and 6 egg whites. Use nonfat milk, nonfat cottage cheese. Reduce the cheddar to ½ cup and use low-fat.

Make it Gluten-Free: Double check and make sure your cheeses are gluten-free. (Most unprocessed cheeses are.)

Make it Vegan: Skip the eggs and instead combine 2 cups of non-dairy milk with 1 cup of silken tofu, 2 tablespoons tahini, and ½ cup nutritional yeast. Combine well in your blender. Use vegan cheeses and refrigerate overnight. Bake at 325 degrees for about 50 minutes.

4 Servings
Calories 302 Total Fat 18.1g Saturated Fat 8.8g Cholesterol 314mg Sodium 630mg Total Carbohydrates 12.4g Dietary Fiber 1.1g Sugars 2.5g Protein 22.2g

This is an impressive dish that is perfect for brunch with friends and family. If you prefer, substitute feta for the goat cheese for a tasty variation.

Goat Cheese, Corn & Zucchini Fritatta

Olive oil spray

1 medium onion, diced fine

2 medium zucchini, diced

2 cups corn kernels, thawed

1 cup cooked quinoa

12 eggs

½ cup milk

½ tsp salt

¼ tsp pepper

¼ tsp cayenne pepper

1 cup low-fat cheddar cheese

4 oz goat cheese

DIRECTIONS:

1. In a large skillet, heat olive oil spray over medium heat. Add onion and zucchini and cook for 10 minutes. Add corn kernels and quinoa and cook for 5 more minutes.

2. Meanwhile, beat eggs and milk in a large bowl. Add in salt, pepper and cayenne.

3. Pour egg mixture over vegetables and quinoa. Add in half of cheddar cheese. Stir until it starts to set and then stop stirring. Top with goat cheese and remaining cheddar and allow to cook until almost done. Lower heat if necessary to prevent browning on the bottom.

4. When the eggs are fully set, place under preheated broiler and cook for 2–3 minutes.

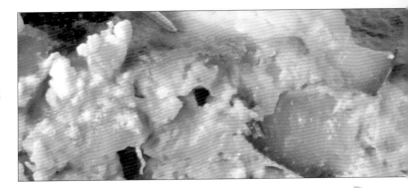

Make it Cleaner: Use nonfat milk and 6 eggs with 12 egg whites. You can skip the cheddar or opt for a reduced amount of low-fat cheddar.

Make it Gluten-Free: As long as you stay away from processed cheeses, this is a great gluten-free way to start your day.

6 servings
Calories 349 Total Fat 18.5g Saturated Fat 8.6g Cholesterol 398mg Sodium 521mg Total Carbohydrates 21.9g Dietary Fiber 3.1g Sugars 5.8g Protein 26.0g

The key to perfectly brown pancakes is a combination of the proper amount of oil on the cooking surface and the proper temperature. If there is too much oil, you will get splotchy pancakes as they will actually fry in the oil. If there is too little heat, you will burn the pancake surface while waiting for the interior batter to cook enough so that the entire pancake can be flipped without it disintegrating into a mash of liquid pancake batter and cooked pancake. If the temperature is too high, you will burn the pancake and make the pancake tough and chewy. The technique I use is to take a small amount of walnut oil and pour it into the middle of the skillet or griddle. I then spread it evenly across the surface with an organic paper towel and wipe off any excess. There should be no depth to the oil and it should merely cover the surface of the skillet or griddle so the pancakes won't stick.

DIRECTIONS:

¾ cup organic all-purpose flour

¾ cup organic quinoa flour

3 ½ tsp baking powder

1 tsp sea salt or Himalayan salt

3 T organic blue agave nectar

1 ¼ cups organic whole milk

1 organic egg

3 T organic butter, melted

2 T organic walnut oil

Organic maple syrup (desired amount)

2 cups of water

1. In a large bowl, sift together the flour, baking powder and salt.

2. After the mixture is thoroughly mixed, make a well in the center and pour in the milk, egg, melted butter and blue agave nectar; mix until smooth.

3. Heat a lightly oiled griddle or frying pan over medium to medium high heat (depending on how your stove is calibrated). Pour or scoop the batter onto the griddle, using approximately ¼ cup for each pancake. The pancake will begin to cook and bubbles will appear on the surface of the pancake. When the center of the pancake is fully bubbled but still in a liquid batter state on top, use a metal spatula and flip the pancake over. If you aren't sure of the calibration of your stove, I recommend lifting up the edge of the pancake for a sneak peek during the cooking process to determine if your temperature is calibrated properly.

4. While the pancakes are cooking, pour the organic maple syrup into a small flat bottomed ramekin, bowl or metal pitcher. Then, place a small skillet or pot on the stove, pour in the water, turn the heat to high and place the container holding the syrup into the skillet or pot so the syrup can heat. When the water begins to boil, turn off the heat.

5. At this point, your pancakes are still cooking. Brown on both sides and serve hot.

6. Pour on syrup and enjoy!

Make it Cleaner: Use whole wheat flour instead of all or part of the white flour. Use skim milk, and 2 egg whites instead of the egg. If you really want to get crazy, skip the butter and use all oil instead.

Make it Vegan: Use 3 T water and 1 T ground flax seed in place of the egg. Allow to simmer on the stove for 5 minutes. Omit the butter and instead use the oil of your choice. Use almond milk (or your favorite non-dairy milk.)

Make it Gluten-Free: Use brown rice flour in place of white flour.

6 servings, nutritional information does not include syrup
Calories 248 Total Fat 11.0g Saturated Fat 4.9g Cholesterol 51mg Sodium 391mg Total Carbohydrates 31.0g Dietary Fiber 3.1g Sugars 5.7g Protein 7.1g

Most health experts agree that whole grains are a great way to start your day. The combination of quinoa and oatmeal takes things to the next level. You get all the benefits of whole grains with an added boost of (complete) protein. Best of all—this one will keep you full until lunchtime.

Quinoa & Oats

1 ½ cups almond milk
(or regular milk if preferred)
¾ cup cooked quinoa
¾ cup old-fashioned oats
¼ tsp salt
½ tsp cinnamon
⅓ cup unsweetened dried cherries
2 T pumpkin seeds
1 T agave nectar (optional)
2 T ground flax seeds (optional)

DIRECTIONS:

1. Combine milk, oats, cinnamon and salt in a saucepan. Bring to boil over high heat. Reduce to medium-low. Add in quinoa and cook for 5–7 minutes.

2. Stir in dried cherries. Place in serving bowls and top with pumpkin seeds. Drizzle with agave nectar and top with ground flax seeds, if desired.

Make it Cleaner: Skip the agave nectar and if you are really watching calories, use water instead of almond milk. Use fresh berries instead of dried. You may also want to leave off the salt if sodium is a concern.

Make it Gluten-Free: Look for gluten-free oats, but first check with your doctor about your specific condition. Some recommend you staying away from oats all together. If so, just skip the oats and either use quinoa flakes (make sure they are gluten-free) or just quinoa!

4 servings
Serving Size 135 g Amount Per Serving Calories 211 Total Fat 5.4g Saturated Fat 1.8g Trans Fat 0.0g Cholesterol 7mg Sodium 189mg Total Carbohydrates 33.1g Dietary Fiber 5.9g Sugars 10.8g Protein 7.8g

My mom loves granola and yogurt, and I came up with this recipe for her. I really like the maple syrup, but you could also use agave nectar. Keep it in an airtight container for up to a week.

Quinoa Berry Granola

DIRECTIONS:

1/3 cup maple syrup

2 T brown sugar

2 T walnut oil

1 1/2 tsp vanilla

1. Preheat oven to 325 degrees.

1/2 cup pumpkin seeds

1/2 cup slivered almonds

1/4 tsp salt

2. In a small bowl, combine maple syrup, brown sugar, walnut oil and vanilla.

1 tsp cinnamon

3. In a large bowl, combine pumpkin seeds, almonds, salt, cinnamon, quinoa and oatmeal.

1 cup quinoa, soaked for 30 minutes

1 cup oatmeal

1/2 cup dried cranberries

4. Toss with maple syrup mixture and spread in a single layer on a baking sheet lined with parchment paper. Bake 25 minutes, stirring every 10 minutes.

1/2 cup tart dried cherries

5. Remove from oven and allow to cool. Stir in dried cranberries and cherries and store in an airtight container.

Make it Cleaner: Skip the brown sugar and instead use 1/2 cup of maple syrup. Make sure your dried fruit is unsweetened or instead add fresh fruit when you eat the granola.

Make it Gluten-Free: If your doctor allows you to eat oatmeal, make sure you choose a gluten-free version. Alternatively, choose gluten-free quinoa flakes.

6 servings
Serving Size 102 g Calories 376 Total Fat 13.3g Saturated Fat 1.7g Trans Fat 0.0g Cholesterol 0mg Sodium 104mg Total Carbohydrates 54.7g Dietary Fiber 5.9g Sugars 19.9g Protein 11.2g

Appetizers

Who knew you could clean up a clean eating recipe and still have it taste delicious? The inspiration for this recipe came from Clean Eating magazine, but here I have made it . . . healthier! The addition of quinoa, basil, red pepper and garlic to the filling means that you have more nutrition and less fat without sacrificing taste. For the sauce, I've used nonfat Greek yogurt and kicked it up a notch with a healthy dose of garlic. If you are not a fan of garlic, feel free to adjust the sauce accordingly.

Goat Cheese Wontons

DIRECTIONS:

1. Preheat oven to 400 degrees. In a medium bowl, combine goat cheese, cooked quinoa, basil, red pepper and garlic.

2. Spread out wonton wrappers on a baking sheet that has been sprayed with olive oil. Put a teaspoon or two of the filling on each wrapper. Brush the edges with water, either using a brush or your fingertips. Fold to form a triangle (or in my case a crescent because I had round wrappers) and press the edges to close. When all of your wrappers are filled (you may use slightly more than ½ of the package of wonton wrappers depending on how full you make them), spray the tops with olive oil spray. Top with parmesan cheese. Bake for 8 to 10 minutes, keeping a close eye on them towards the end. The wontons are done when they are a golden brown.

3. To make the roasted red pepper sauce, combine red peppers, yogurt, basil, garlic, sea salt and pepper in your blender. Process until well blended.

6 oz (½ package) wonton wrappers (whole wheat if you can find them)
4 oz goat cheese
1 cup cooked quinoa
1 T basil, chopped fine
⅛–¼ tsp crushed red pepper
3 cloves garlic, minced
Olive oil cooking spray
¼ cup fresh parmesan, grated
½ cup roasted red peppers
½ cup nonfat Greek yogurt
2 T basil, chopped
6 cloves garlic, minced
½ tsp sea salt
¼ tsp black pepper

Note: Make sure that you use Greek yogurt and not traditional in the sauce. Greek yogurt is much thicker and gives the sauce the correct consistency. I really like Fage, but there are a number of good brands on the market.

Make it Vegan: If you are a vegan, use vegan cheese and make your own Greek-like yogurt. Place vegan yogurt in a fine metal sieve over a bowl and allow it to drain in your refrigerator overnight.

Serves 6
Serving Size 119 g Calories 300 Total Fat 9.9g Saturated Fat 5.6g Cholesterol 30mg Sodium 506mg Total Carbohydrates 35.6g Dietary Fiber 2.7g Sugars 2.3g Protein 16.5g

This works well as an appetizer or a main course. The quinoa adds substance, but you will hardly know it is there. Traditional spanakopita relies on butter between the layers but I've lightened this dish by using olive oil spray. The phyllo dough will tear, so don't panic! It will still come out great!

Quinoa Spanakopita

Olive oil spray
1 red onion, chopped fine
6 oz fresh spinach
1 ½ cups cooked quinoa
¼ cup fresh chopped parsley
1 tsp salt
¼ tsp fresh ground pepper
8 oz feta, cubed
1 egg, beaten
12 oz phyllo dough
Olive oil or olive oil spray,
for brushing or spraying
(NOT PAM! USE A MISTO OR BRUSH!)

DIRECTIONS:

1. Preheat oven to 350 degrees. Heat olive oil spray over medium heat. Add diced onion and cook for 8 minutes. Add in spinach and cook until it begins to wilt. Add in quinoa and cook until the spinach is fully wilted. Remove from heat and season with salt and pepper. Stir in parsley. Allow to cool slightly and combine with feta and beaten egg.

2. Roll out 1 sheet of phyllo dough. Spray or brush with olive oil and add another sheet. Spray or brush again and cut lengthwise. Place 1 tablespoon of filling and fold over to form a triangle. Continue folding in a triangle shape. Place seam side down on a prepared baking sheet. Spray or brush with olive oil. Continue with remaining phyllo dough and filling.

3. Bake for 20–25 minutes, until golden brown.

Make it Cleaner: Use 2 egg whites instead of the egg. Use low-fat feta and reduce the amount by half, increasing the amount of spinach by 3 oz.

Make it Vegan: Substitute 8 ounces of crumbled extra firm tofu and 2 tablespoons of nutritional yeast for the feta. In place of the egg combine 1 tablespoon of ground flax seeds mixed with 2 tablespoons of water. Allow to sit for 10 minutes before proceeding.

Make it Quick: If prep time is tight, turn it into a casserole! Spray a 13 x 9 pan with olive oil spray and layer with 8 layers of dough, spraying between each layer. Spread filling and top with remaining dough, again spraying between each layer. Spray the top and bake for 45 minutes at 375 degrees.

Make it Gluten-Free: Skip the phyllo dough altogether. Instead, turn the dish into a casserole and use the gluten-free pie crust of your choice as a topper.

Serves 12 (Nutritional Data based on 2 T of olive oil used)
Serving Size 85 g Calories 192 Total Fat 8.8g Saturated Fat 3.7g Cholesterol 32mg Sodium 559mg Total Carbohydrates 21.5g Dietary Fiber 1.5g Sugars 1.3g Protein 6.6g

This dish is easy to make and surprisingly delicious! Even my husband, who isn't a fan of whole tomatoes, enjoyed this one! It is especially great in the summer when tomatoes are at their best!

DIRECTIONS:

1. Preheat oven to 450 degrees.

2. Place tomatoes upside down on paper towels to drain.

3. Combine breadcrumbs, quinoa, green onions, parmesan cheese, thyme, garlic, salt and pepper. Place mixture inside tomatoes. Sprinkle with mozzarella cheese.

4. Lightly grease a 13 x 9 baking dish. Bake for 10 minutes at 450 degrees.

6 plum tomatoes, cut in half lengthwise and seeded

½ cup panko breadcrumbs

½ cup cooked quinoa

⅓ cup green onions, chopped

⅓ cup fresh parmesan cheese, grated

⅓ cup low-fat mozzarella

1 T fresh thyme, chopped

4 cloves garlic, minced

½ tsp salt

½ tsp pepper

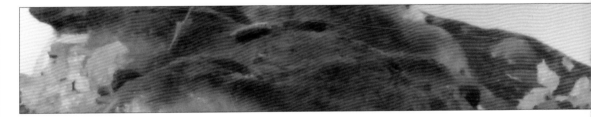

Make it Quick: Make the filling ahead of time and store in the refrigerator for up to 2 days. The filling may also be frozen.

Make it Vegan: Use vegan cheese instead of mozzarella and parmesan or skip the cheese altogether and spray olive oil over the breadcrumb and quinoa mixture. A sprinkling of nutritional yeast would also be nice.

Make it Cleaner: Use whole wheat breadcrumbs. Make them yourself by chopping leftover whole grain bread in your food processor. Spray olive oil on a baking sheet and bake for 15 to 20 minutes, stirring often, until golden brown. You could also skip the cheese and follow the directions to make it vegan above.

Make it Gluten-Free : Make sure your cheeses are unprocessed and gluten-free. Use gluten-free bread and follow the directions above to make your own breadcrumbs. You can also make breadcrumbs by combining bread processed in your food processor with a few tablespoons of olive oil. Heat a skillet over medium-high heat and cook breadcrumbs for 7 to 9 minutes, stirring often to prevent burning. Reduce heat to medium and cook for another 5 minutes until brown. Make extra and store in the freezer for up to 3 months so you always have gluten-free breadcrumbs on hand.

Serving Size 155 g
Amount Per Serving Calories 117 Calories from Fat 32 Total Fat 3.6g Saturated Fat 1.8g Trans Fat 0.0g Cholesterol 8mg Sodium 337mg Total Carbohydrates 15.7g Dietary Fiber 2.7g Sugars 5.3g Protein 7.2g

This is a dish that can be enjoyed as an appetizer or the main course! Serve it with crusty whole wheat artisan bread and you have a dish that is special enough for company!

Quinoa with Marinated Olives & Goat Cheese

1 ½ cups marinated black and green olives
1 T olive oil
Zest of 1 lemon
Zest of ½ orange
4 cloves minced garlic
1 tsp dried thyme
2 bay leaves
2 cups cooked quinoa
Juice of 1 lemon
Juice of ½ orange
1 cup grape tomatoes, sliced
4 oz goat cheese
French bread for serving (optional)

DIRECTIONS:

1. Place olives, olive oil, lemon zest, orange zest, garlic, thyme and bay leaves over low heat in a saucepan. Cook for 5 minutes. Raise heat to medium-low. Stir in quinoa, lemon juice, orange juice and tomatoes. Cook for 4–6 minutes, until tomatoes are tender. Remove bay leaves.

2. Crumble goat cheese on top of olive mixture and serve with French bread slices, if desired.

Make it Cleaner: Skip the bread and enjoy the olives in moderation.

Make it Vegan: Skip the goat cheese and instead use a small cube of vegan cheese. I like Daiya cheddar or mozarella-style cheeses!

Make it Gluten-Free: Opt for gluten-free bread and make sure that the olives you buy do not have any hidden gluten. Typically they wouldn't, but often these preparations are made in-house, so it is always a good idea to read labels or ask.

Serving Size 103 g
Amount Per Serving Calories 266 Total Fat 19.0g Saturated Fat 3.8g Cholesterol 15mg Sodium 731mg Total Carbohydrates 17.0g Dietary Fiber 4.1g Sugars 1.7g Protein 6.6g

If you have never tried hummus with quinoa you are missing out! The quinoa blends in perfectly, adding smoothness and substance. I have to admit I was very skeptical when I first heard the idea but I've tried it so many times that I never make hummus without it! One of the keys to smooth, rich tasting hummus is to start with warm chickpeas (often called garbanzo beans). The heat helps the flavors blend and also helps to cut the acidity of the garlic. Instead of water, you can also substitute the cooking liquid from the beans or the liquid from the can. This is a great basic hummus recipe, so feel free to substitute ingredients to suit your tastes. Roasted red peppers, olives, cilantro and parsley are all fantastic alternatives.

Sun-Dried Tomato Hummus

3 cups cooked chickpeas,
warm (2 15-oz cans)

¼ cup lemon juice

6 cloves minced garlic

6 sun-dried tomatoes, chopped

1 cup cooked quinoa

¹/₃ cup tahini

¼–½ tsp cayenne pepper

¹/₃ cup of water, as needed

DIRECTIONS:

1. Puree warm chickpeas, lemon juice, garlic, tomatoes and quinoa in your food processor for 4 minutes. Add tahini and cayenne pepper and process 2 more minutes, adding additional water (or cooking liquid) to achieve the desired texture.

Make it Quick: Cook a batch of plain quinoa once a week so that you have it on hand whenever you want to make a quick salad, casserole or in dishes like this one. It will last for a week in the refrigerator and can also be frozen for up to 3 months. If you are really short on time, skip cooking your own chickpeas, which takes both time and planning ahead. Use BPA-free chickpeas and pre-minced garlic.

12 servings
Serving Size 86 g Amount Per Serving Calories 134 Total Fat 4.8g Saturated Fat 0.6g Cholesterol 0mg Sodium 192mg Total Carbohydrates 19.1g Dietary Fiber 3.7g Protein 4.9g

I've always made my own trail mix by combining ingredients from the bulk bins at Whole Foods. Recently, I was browsing through an old issue of Vegetarian Times *and came across a recipe for spiced nuts. It gave me the idea of spicing up my trail mix and the following recipe was born.*

Sweet & Spicy Trail Mix

2 tsp ground cumin
1 tsp sweet paprika
½ tsp cayenne pepper
1 tsp garlic powder
1 cup quinoa
1 cup raw sunflower seeds
1 cup raw cashews
1 cup raw walnuts
3 T olive oil
3 T coconut palm sugar
1 cup dried cranberries (optional)

DIRECTIONS:

1. Preheat the oven to 325 degrees. Combine cumin, paprika, cayenne pepper and garlic in a small bowl.

2. Combine quinoa, sunflower seeds, cashews and walnuts in a medium bowl. Toss with olive oil and coconut palm sugar and add in spices. Stir until well combined. If desired, season to taste with mineral sea salt.

3. Spread on baking sheets and bake for 30 minutes, stirring every 10 minutes.

4. Allow to cool and stir in dried cranberries if desired.

 Make it Cleaner: Reduce both olive oil and sugar to 2 tablespoons.

Serving Size 55 g
Amount Per Serving Calories 238 Calories from Fat 159 Total Fat 17.7g Saturated Fat 2.1g Cholesterol 0mg Sodium 4mg Total Carbohydrates 15.5g Dietary Fiber 2.8g Sugars 1.2g Protein 7.1g

Soups
& Salads

If you are looking for a quinoa salad recipe to win over the quinoa skeptic, this is a great place to start. Packed with flavor, this is a favorite around our house.

Balsamic Quinoa Salad

½ cup balsamic vinegar
¼–½ cup best quality extra-virgin olive oil (depending on if you are watching calories)
2 T Dijon mustard
6 cloves of garlic, minced
2 shallots, minced
Salt, pepper and cayenne pepper, to taste
1 ½ cups quinoa
Bouillon cube
5 sun-dried tomatoes (not in oil)
1 red pepper, chopped
4 oz blue cheese
1 can black beans (or 2 cups)

DIRECTIONS:

1. Make dressing by combining vinegar, mustard, garlic, shallots and olive oil. Season to taste.

2. Add quinoa to 3 cups of boiling water. Boil for 10 minutes.

3. Rinse with cool water and place in a fine mesh colander. Boil water and place quinoa and sun-dried tomatoes in the colander over the water. Cover with a kitchen towel and lid. Steam for 10 minutes. Allow to cool.

4. Cook red pepper in a small skillet until tender.

5. Combine pepper and remaining ingredients with quinoa. Add dressing (I typically only use ⅓ cup of the dressing and save the rest for leftovers and salad) and toss. Enjoy!

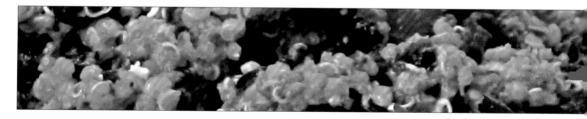

 Make it Cleaner: Skip the olive oil and instead combine 1 tablespoon chia seeds with ½ cup water. Allow to sit for 15 minutes and then proceed as directed.

Make it Vegan: Use the vegan cheese of your choosing!

Serves 8
Calories 312 Carbohydrates 37g Protein 12g Fat 13.78g Cholesterol 10.73 mg Fiber 6.93g

This slaw is quite the variation from your traditional slaw. Shredded cabbages, quinoa, and thinly sliced red onions and radishes are off-set by a dressing that has quite a bit of bite. If you really want to take things up a notch, add extra garlic!

Cabbage & Radish Slaw

2 cups green cabbage, shredded
2 cups purple cabbage, shredded
2 cups cooked quinoa
1 red onion, sliced thin
4 radishes, sliced thin
¼ cup fresh cilantro, chopped
Juice of 2 limes
¼ cup raw apple cider vinegar
¼ cup red wine vinegar
2 T olive oil
2 cloves garlic, minced
¼ tsp crushed red pepper
1 tsp caraway seeds

DIRECTIONS:

1. Combine cabbages, quinoa, red onion and radishes in a large bowl.

2. In a small bowl, combine lime juice, apple cider vinegar, red wine vinegar, olive oil, garlic, caraway seeds and crushed red pepper. Salt and pepper to taste.

3. Toss dressing with the cabbage mixture and serve.

Make it Quick: Using your food processor to shred the cabbage is a real time saver. If I'm really short on time I will run the radishes through as well! Alternatively, you can buy coleslaw mix.

Make it Gluten-Free: Vinegars are typically gluten-free, but it doesn't hurt to check!

Make it Cleaner: Skip the olive oil and use 2 tablespoons of chia gel. To make it, combine ⅓ cup chia seeds with 2 cups of water. Pulse in your blender and allow to sit for 20 minutes, pulsing every 5 minutes or so. Store for up to a week in the refrigerator and use 1:1 as a replacement for all or part of the olive oil in any salad dressing recipe you choose.

6 servings
Calories 133 Total Fat 5.7g Saturated Fat 0.8g Trans Fat 0.0g Cholesterol 0mg Sodium 13mg Total Carbohydrates 17.1g Dietary Fiber 3.0g Sugars 2.5g

If you have never tried white balsamic vinegar, it is a great alternative to white wine vinegar. Light and flavorful, it really adds a punch to this salad.

Corn & Quinoa Salad

DIRECTIONS:

1. Combine quinoa, corn, tomatoes and pepper in a medium bowl.

2. In a small bowl or salad dressing mixer, combine shallots, vinegar, mustard, sea salt and pepper. Slowly add in olive oil.

3. Toss quinoa mixture with arugula and toss with dressing. Top with basil, goat cheese and almonds.

2 cups cooked quinoa
3 cups of corn (fresh preferred, but thawed frozen will work)
2 cups grape tomatoes, halved
1 red pepper, chopped
6 cups arugula or baby spinach
1/3 cup fresh basil, sliced
3 oz goat cheese, crumbled
1/4 cup slivered almonds
Dressing
3 shallots, finely diced
3 T white balsamic vinegar
1 T Dijon mustard
1 tsp mineral sea salt
1/2 tsp ground black pepper
2 T extra-virgin olive oil

Make it Vegan: Use the vegan cheese of your choice.

Make it Gluten-Free: Double check your mustard to ensure that it is gluten-free!

Make it Cleaner: Use chia gel in place of the olive oil. To make it, combine 1/3 cup chia seeds with 2 cups of water. Pulse in your blender and allow to sit for 20 minutes, pulsing every 5 minutes or so. Store for up to a week in the refrigerator and use 1:1 as a replacement for all or part of the olive oil in any salad dressing recipe you choose.

Make it Quick: Purchase a prepared balsamic vinegar dressing or prepare this one ahead of time. Use frozen corn (thawed), purchase washed spinach or arugula.

6 servings
Calories 286 Total Fat 13.9g Saturated Fat 4.6g Trans Fat 0.0g Cholesterol 15mg Sodium 413mg Total Carbohydrates 32.3g Dietary Fiber 5.3g Sugars 5.5g Protein 11.6g

Ready for a fiesta? Here's how to do it healthy! This nutritious quinoa salad is fun, beautiful and, most importantly, delicious. The first time I made this my husband was sure he was going to hate it. As it turns out, it is one of his favorite recipes!

Fiesta Quinoa Salad

1 cup of quinoa, rinsed
2 cups of chicken or vegetable broth
1 15-oz can of corn, drained
1 red pepper, chopped
3 scallions, chopped
¾ cup dried cranberries
¾ cup carrots, chopped
3 T fresh cilantro
4 T red onion, divided
3 cloves garlic, minced
4 T soy sauce
2 T lemon juice
½ cup olive oil
1 tsp cumin
$1/8$ tsp dried chipotle pepper
¼ cup raw almonds, chopped and toasted (or pine nuts) (optional—not included in nutrition data)
¼ cup roasted pumpkin seeds (optional—not included in nutrition data)

DIRECTIONS:

1. Cook the quinoa using the stovetop steaming method. Bring the broth to a boil and add in quinoa and salt to taste. Boil for 10 minutes. Drain quinoa and rinse with cool water. Rinse the pot and bring fresh water to a boil. Place quinoa in a metal colander and put over the boiling water. Cover with a clean dish cloth and lid. Steam for 10 minutes. Remove from heat and allow the quinoa to cool. (Alternatively, you could also cook the quinoa in a vegetable steamer.)

2. Meanwhile, in a large bowl, mix together corn, red pepper, scallions, cranberries, carrots, cilantro and 2 T of the red onion.

3. In your blender, combine remaining 1 T of red onion, garlic, soy sauce, lemon juice, olive oil, cumin and dried chipotle pepper. Pulse until well combined.

4. Combine quinoa and vegetable mixture and toss with dressing. Top with almonds and pumpkin seeds

Serves 6 as a Main Course
Calories 406 Carbohydrates 50.15 Protein 8.9g Fat 21.28g Saturated Fat 2.95g Cholesterol 0mg Fiber 5.86g

I've used the balsamic walnuts here because honestly I just can't get enough of them! Mixed with goat cheese and raspberries, this is sure to please the most demanding of your friends and family! If raspberries are not in season, feel free to substitute another fruit. Blueberries, strawberries and even green apples would all work beautifully. Make it a meal with some whole wheat crusty bread spread with a little goat cheese!

Goat Cheese, Raspberry & Balsamic Walnut Salad

Walnuts
3 T agave nectar
1 T balsamic vinegar
¾ cup walnuts

Salad
7 oz baby arugula
¾ cup raspberries
4 oz goat cheese
1 cup cooked quinoa

Dressing
2 T shallots, minced
4 large cloves of garlic, minced
(more or less to your taste)
2 tsp Dijon mustard
¼ cup balsamic vinegar
¼ cup extra-virgin olive oil
¼ tsp cayenne pepper
Freshly ground black pepper and
mineral sea salt, to taste

DIRECTIONS:

1. Make the dressing: Place minced shallots and garlic in a small bowl and combine with Dijon mustard. Add balsamic vinegar, cayenne pepper, salt and pepper. Slowly pour in olive oil to the mixture, mixing as you go. You almost want to go drop by drop. The goal is to create a creamy emulsified dressing. The dressing will keep in the refrigerator for at least 4 days.

2. Make the walnuts: Preheat oven to 350 degrees. Stir together vinegar and agave nectar in a small microwave-safe bowl. Heat on high in the microwave for 1 minute. Toss walnuts in vinegar mixture. Place on a baking sheet lined with parchment paper and cook for 10 minutes.

3. In a large bowl, combine arugula, raspberries, goat cheese and cooked quinoa. Toss with desired amount of dressing and top with walnuts.

Make it Cleaner: Skip the olive oil in the dressing and instead use chia gel. To make it, combine ⅓ cup chia seeds with 2 cups of water. Pulse in your blender and allow to sit for 20 minutes, pulsing every 5 minutes or so. Store for up to a week in the refrigerator and use 1:1 as a replacement for all or part of the olive oil in any salad dressing recipe you choose.

Make it Vegan: Skip the goat cheese and instead use your favorite nut cheese.

Make it Gluten-Free: Be sure to make sure that the mustard you are using is gluten-free!

Calories 331 Total Fat 25.9g Saturated Fat 6.5g Trans Fat 0.0g Cholesterol 20mg Sodium 96mg Total Carbohydrates 15.2g Dietary Fiber 3.5g Sugars 4.9g Protein 12.1g

This healthy and delicious quinoa salad is perfect for breakfast or lunch. It also makes a great side dish for a more hearty meal. I have to say that this is one of my favorite vegan quinoa salad recipes!

Jeweled Quinoa Salad

½ tsp ground turmeric
1 T olive oil
4 green onions, chopped
1 cup quinoa, rinsed
3 tsp garlic, minced
1 bay leaf
2 T dried apricots
2 T dried cranberries
2 T dried raisins
¼ cup pistachios, chopped
1 T lemon juice

DIRECTIONS:

1. Combine turmeric with 1 ½ cups hot water and stir until dissolved.

2. Heat olive oil in a saucepan. Add green onions and quinoa and sauté for 3 minutes. Add garlic and cook 1 more minute. Pour turmeric water over quinoa. Add bay leaf and salt and pepper to taste.

3. Bring to a simmer and reduce to low. Cover and cook 25 to 30 minutes. Remove from heat. Fold in fruits and cover. Allow to sit for 5 minutes. Stir in pistachios, green onion and lemon juice and enjoy!

Calories 249 Total Fat 9.5g Protein 7.9g

This soup is light, but also very filling. It is perfect for those times when you are feeling low and need the comfort of a healthy soup.

Quinoa Black Bean Soup

DIRECTIONS:

1. Heat oil over medium heat. Add onion and pepper and sauté for 5 minutes. Add quinoa, garlic and chili powder and sauté another 3 minutes.

2. Stir in broth, beans, carrots, corn, bay leaf and 2 cups of water. Season with salt and pepper.

3. Bring to a boil. Reduce heat to medium-low and simmer covered for 20 minutes. Stir in cilantro and lime juice. Top with green onions and cheddar cheese, if desired.

1 T olive oil
1 onion, chopped
1 red bell pepper, chopped
6 cloves garlic, minced
¾ cup quinoa, rinsed
1 ½ tsp chili powder
2 ½ cups vegetable broth
2 cups (or 1 15-oz can) of black beans
1 cup grated carrots
1 cup corn kernels
1 bay leaf
¼ cup chopped cilantro
2 T lime juice
Salt and pepper to taste
Thinly sliced green onions and
cheddar cheese, for topping

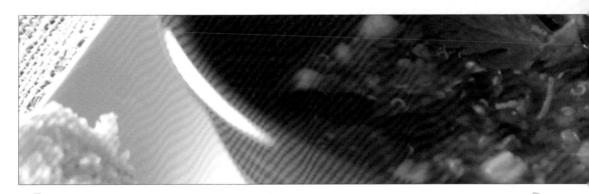

Make it Cleaner: Skip the olive oil and use olive oil spray.

Make it Vegan: Instead of topping with cheddar cheese try toasting a few corn tortillas and cutting them into thin slices.

Make it Gluten-Free: Make sure to choose gluten-free broth.

Make it Quick: Used canned black beans and purchased pre-cut onion, peppers and grated carrots.

Serving Size 177 g
Amount Per Serving Calories 176 Total Fat 3.7g Saturated Fat 0.6g Trans Fat 0.0g Cholesterol 0mg Sodium 259mg Total Carbohydrates 28.5g Dietary Fiber 5.2g Sugars 3.2g Protein 8.4g

Somehow I made it until now without ever trying beets—don't ask me how! I was a little nervous, but this was delicious and my husband especially enjoyed it.

Roasted Beet Quinoa Salad with Poppy Seed Dressing

2 bunches of beets
2 cups of cooked quinoa
1 ½ cups arugula
1 ½ cups watercress
½ red onion, sliced thin
4 oz goat cheese
Poppy Seed Dressing
2 T apple cider vinegar
2 T walnut oil
2 T nonfat Greek yogurt
1 tsp poppy seeds
2 tsp agave nectar
1 tsp mineral sea salt
4 cloves garlic, minced

DIRECTIONS:

1. Preheat oven to 375 degrees.

2. Trim and wash beets. Place in large baking dish and cover with foil. Bake at 375 degrees for 1 ½ hours or until tender. Cool; peel and thinly slice.

3. Combine arugula and watercress and divide between 4 serving dishes. Top with ¼ onion, beets, quinoa and goat cheese. Drizzle with poppy seed dressing.

Poppy Seed Dressing

1. Combine all ingredients in a small bowl and blend with a whisk until well combined.

6 Servings
Serving Size 2 T Amount Per Serving Calories 27 Total Fat 1.8g Trans Fat 0.0g Cholesterol 0mg Sodium 314mg Total Carbohydrates 2.0g Sugars 0.9g Protein 1.1g

Make it Vegan: Use cashews instead of the goat cheese and choose a vegan yogurt.

Make it Gluten-Free: Make sure the yogurt you select is gluten-free.

Make it Quick: Roast the beets ahead of time and store them peeled and sliced in the refrigerator. Buy diced red onions. You may also make the dressing a day ahead.

Make it Cleaner: Skip the goat cheese.

Serving Size 135 g
Calories 190 Total Fat 8.0g Saturated Fat 4.8g Cholesterol 20mg Sodium 130mg Total Carbohydrates 20.5g Dietary Fiber 3.0g Sugars 6.9g Protein 10.0g

This soup is so rich, you will forget that it is at all healthy. Perfect for those cool autumn nights when you just need a little comfort food.

Roasted Butternut Squash Soup with Goat Cheese Toasts

2 ½ lb butternut squash (1 large)
Olive oil spray
1 T walnut oil
1 onion, chopped
6 cloves garlic, minced
6 cups vegetable stock
1 cup of quinoa, rinsed
1 T chopped fresh sage
¾ tsp salt
½ tsp fresh ground black pepper
1 bay leaf
6 oz French baguette
2 oz goat cheese
2 T chives

DIRECTIONS:

1. Preheat oven to 400 degrees.

2. Cut squash in half and discard seeds. Place cut-side down on a foil-lined cookie sheet coated with olive oil spray. Bake for 30 minutes. Cool slightly and scoop squash into a bowl. Discard peel. Mash pulp.

3. Heat a pan over medium-high heat. Add oil. Add onion and sauté for 4 minutes. Add garlic and cook another 30 seconds. Add squash, vegetable stock, quinoa, sage, salt, pepper and bay leaf. Bring to a boil.

4. Reduce heat and simmer for 45 minutes, stirring occasionally. Remove from heat and discard bay leaf. Allow to cool slightly.

5. Preheat broiler. Slice baguette and place on a baking sheet. Cover with goat cheese and chives and broil for 2 minutes.

6. Place ⅓ of vegetable mixture into food processor or blender. Process until smooth. Pour into a large bowl and repeat with remaining mixture. (Alternatively, use a hand blender to puree.) Return pureed mixture to pan and cook over medium heat for 3 minutes.

Make it Gluten-Free: Choose a gluten-free bread and make sure that your vegetable stock is gluten-free.

Make it Vegan: Choose vegan bread and in place of goat cheese choose the vegan cheese of your choice. Or use softened tofu sprinkled with a bit of nutritional yeast.

Make it Cleaner: Skip the toasts and just enjoy the soup!

Make it Quick: Purchase peeled and cubed squash and roast for 20 minutes. Buy pre-cut onion and minced garlic. Making the soup ahead is also a great option.

Serves 8
Serving Size 379 g Amount Per Serving Calories 258 Total Fat 5.1g Saturated Fat 2.1g Cholesterol 7mg Sodium 473mg Total Carbohydrates 45.5g Dietary fiber 6.1g Sugars 5.6g Protein 10.2g

Southwestern Quinoa Salad

3 cups of water
Vegetable bouillon cube
1 ½ cups of quinoa, rinsed
½ tsp sea salt (optional)
Juice from 3 limes
2 tsp cumin
½ tsp chili powder
$^1/_8$ tsp ground chipotle chili powder (or cayenne)
2 T red wine vinegar
2 T olive oil
4 cloves of minced garlic
1 can black beans, drained
½ cup fresh or frozen corn (steam the corn if using fresh)
½ red onion, diced
½ cup roasted red pepper, diced
1 T minced jalapeños
¼ cup cilantro
½ cup queso fresco (optional)
Salt and pepper to taste

DIRECTIONS:

1. In a large pot, combine water and vegetable bouillon and bring to a boil. Add quinoa and salt and boil for 10 minutes.

2. Remove from heat. Return quinoa to the pot and cover. Allow to sit for 10 minutes.

3. Meanwhile, make the dressing by combining lime juice, cumin, chili powder, chipotle chili powder, vinegar, olive oil and garlic. (You can do this in a small bowl or in a blender.)

4. In a separate bowl, combine black beans, corn, onion, red pepper, jalapeños and cilantro.

5. After quinoa cools slightly, combine with black bean mixture. Stir in cheese, if desired.

6. Toss with dressing and serve at room temperature or chilled.

Serves 8
Calories 228 Carbohydrate 37.5g Protein 8.75g Fat 5.72g Cholesterol .07 mg Fiber 6.34g

If you choose to make just one salad recipe out of the book, this one would be my pick. The dressing is absolutely delicious! Since avocado tends to spoil so quickly after it is cut I wasn't expecting the dressing to still be good the next day, but surprisingly it was. I can't tell you if it lasts beyond that because it's never gotten that far in my house.

Southwestern Salad with Jalapeño Avocado Dressing

6 cups mixed greens
1 cup black beans, drained
1 cup corn, drained
1 cup cooked quinoa
3 plum tomatoes, seeded and diced
1 red pepper, seeded and diced
1 red onion, sliced
2 T red wine vinegar
½ cup shredded cheese
Creamy Jalapeño Avocado Dressing
2 jalapeños, seeded and diced
6 cloves garlic
1 avocado
1 cup cilantro
1 cup nonfat Greek yogurt
4 scallions, chopped
2 T fresh lime juice
1 T red wine vinegar
1 tsp mineral sea salt
½ tsp fresh ground black pepper

DIRECTIONS:

1. Soak red onion in red wine vinegar for 30 minutes to 2 hours. (Note: this step is optional and can be skipped if you are in a hurry. Alternatively, you can soak in a covered dish overnight in the refrigerator.)

2. Combine ingredients and toss with Creamy Jalapeño Avocado Dressing.

Creamy Jalapeño Avocado Dressing

1. Combine ingredients in a food processor until well blended. Use nonfat milk as needed to reach desired consistency. (Dressing will be thick and is best tossed.)

Make it Vegan: Use vegan cheese and yogurt.

Make it Gluten-Free: This dish is naturally gluten-free.

Make it Cleaner: Quite honestly, I think this dish is just about as clean as it gets!

Make it Quick: Buy bagged greens and pre-cut peppers and onions. Cook quinoa once a week so that you always have some on hand for dishes like this one. Used pickled diced jalapeños instead of fresh, and purchase a tube of cilantro rather than washing and chopping fresh cilantro.

Serves 6
Serving Size 205g Amount Per Serving Calories 128 Total Fat 1.3g Trans Fat 0.0g Cholesterol 0mg Sodium 20mg Total Carbohydrates 25.0g Dietary Fiber 5.0g Sugars 6.2g Protein 6.1g

This quinoa salad is the perfect solution to your busy week! As a work at home, homeschooling mom, one thing that saves me time and again is making a big batch of quinoa on the weekend. Starting with cooked quinoa, dishes like this come together in a matter of minutes. Healthy and delicious, this is a recipe you will reach for time and again!

Spicy Quinoa Salad

DIRECTIONS:

1. In a large bowl, combine quinoa, corn, red pepper and cilantro.

2. In a small bowl, combine lime juice, olive oil, garlic, chipotle chili powder, smoked paprika and salt.

3. Toss dressing with quinoa mixture and serve at room temperature or chilled.

3 cups cooked quinoa (1 cup uncooked)
2 cups corn
1 red pepper, chopped
2 T fresh cilantro, chopped
2 T fresh lime juice
½ T olive oil
2 cloves garlic, minced
¼ tsp chipotle chili powder
½ tsp smoked paprika
½ tsp salt

Serves 4
Amount Per Serving Calories 243 Total Fat 5.2g Total Carbohydrates 43.4g Dietary Fiber 5.7g Protein 8.6g

I love fruit on a salad and this is one of my favorites. Strawberries, oranges, goat cheese and almonds—what could be better? This dressing is delicious and easy to make and would work well on just about any salad. If you like poppy seed dressing, don't miss this salad!

Strawberry Spinach Quinoa Salad

6 cups spinach
1 cup cooked quinoa
1 red onion, sliced thin
2 T red wine vinegar
3 fresh mandarin oranges ("cuties"),
peeled and cut into sections
10 strawberries, sliced
¼ cup slivered almonds
2 oz goat cheese
Raspberry Poppy Seed Vinaigrette
1 T poppy seeds
2 T raspberry vinegar
¼ cup orange juice
1 tsp agave nectar (use 2 if you like
sweet dressings)
1 T Dijon mustard
1 shallot, minced
3 T olive oil
½ tsp salt
¼ tsp paprika

DIRECTIONS:

1. Slice onions and place in a small bowl. Top with red wine vinegar and allow to marinate for at least 30 minutes or several hours.

2. In a large bowl, combine spinach, quinoa, marinated red onion, oranges and strawberries. Toss with Raspberry Poppy Seed Vinaigrette and top with almonds and goat cheese.

Raspberry Poppy Seed Vinaigrette

1. Combine all ingredients in a blender and process until well combined.

Serves 6
Serving Size 29 g Calories 78 Total Fat 7.5g Saturated Fat 1.0g Trans Fat 0.0g Cholesterol 0mg Sodium 224mg Total Carbohydrates 2.3g Sugars 1.5g Protein 0.5g

{ Make it Vegan: Skip the goat cheese and add additional almonds.

Make it Cleaner: Skip the goat cheese and make sure your orange juice is from a fresh-squeezed orange. Use chia gel in place of the olive oil in your dressing. To make it, combine 1/3 cup chia seeds with 2 cups of water. Pulse in your blender and allow to sit for 20 minutes, pulsing every 5 minutes or so. Store for up to a week in the refrigerator and use 1:1 as a replacement for all or part of the olive oil in any salad dressing recipe you choose.

Make it Gluten-Free: Vinegars are traditionally gluten-free, but make sure you check. Opt for a gluten-free mustard.

Make it Quick: Prepare the dressing a day ahead of time, or purchase a prepared poppy seed dressing. Buy diced onions and washed spinach. You may also want to use canned mandarin oranges. }

Serves 6
Calories 166 Total Fat 6.1g Saturated Fat 2.6g Trans Fat 0.0g Cholesterol 10mg Sodium 64mg Total Carbohydrates 23.1g Dietary Fiber 3.3g Sugars 13.3g Protein 6.9g

Entrees & Sides

This recipe was inspired by Cooks Illustrated *and is a light way to enjoy tostadas that doesn't sacrifice flavor. The addition of quinoa to the mix helps make the dish more filling and also adds a nice texture. If you prefer, try this with red, yellow and green pepper instead of just red! I used the Mexican Quinoa from this cookbook and it was fabulous!*

Black Bean & Quinoa Tostadas

DIRECTIONS:

1. Preheat the oven to 450 degrees. Spread tortillas on 2 baking sheets and coat with oil spray on each side. Bake 8 to 10 minutes, until crisp. Rotate baking sheets after 4 minutes.

2. Put 1 T olive oil in a large skillet over medium-low heat and add onions and peppers. Cook covered for 10 minutes. Uncover and increase heat to medium high. Cook for 6 more minutes. Add garlic and cook for an additional 30 seconds.

3. Remove from heat and stir in 1 T lime juice. Salt and pepper to taste.

4. Heat remaining 1 T of olive oil in skillet. Add beans, jalapeños and 1 T of the brine. Cook for 5 minutes, mashing beans with the back of your fork or a potato masher.

5. Toss coleslaw mix with remaining jalapeño brine. Season with salt and pepper.

6. In a small bowl, combine yogurt, cilantro and garlic.

7. Spread beans on tortillas, and top with quinoa, vegetables and slaw. Top with yogurt mixture and sprinkle queso fresco.

12 6-inch corn tortillas
Olive oil spray
3 red peppers, seeded and sliced thin
2 onions, sliced thin
2 T olive oil
6 cloves garlic, minced
3 T lime juice
4 cups black beans (2 cans)
1 T chopped jarred jalapeños plus ¼ cup brine
1 bag broccoli slaw
2 cups cooked quinoa
2 oz queso fresco
½ cup nonfat Greek yogurt
2 T fresh cilantro, minced
3 cloves garlic, minced

 Make it Vegan: Use vegan yogurt. Instead of topping with queso fresco, try some pepitas with a dash of nutritional yeast.

Serving Size 131 g
Amount Per Serving Calories 217 Total Fat 4.4g Saturated Fat 0.8g Trans Fat 0.0g Cholesterol 2mg Sodium 54mg Total Carbohydrates 35.6g Dietary Fiber 6.6g Sugars 2.9g Protein 10.3g

I realize that while I love lentils, not everyone does. If you are looking for a great veggie burger recipe that doesn't have lentils, this is one of the best ones I've tried. Six cloves of garlic may seem like a lot to you, but if you like garlic, I encourage you to give it a try! The garlic combined with the chipotle chili really gives these burgers a kick! Of course, if you aren't nuts over garlic like I am, make sure you adjust to suit your tastes.

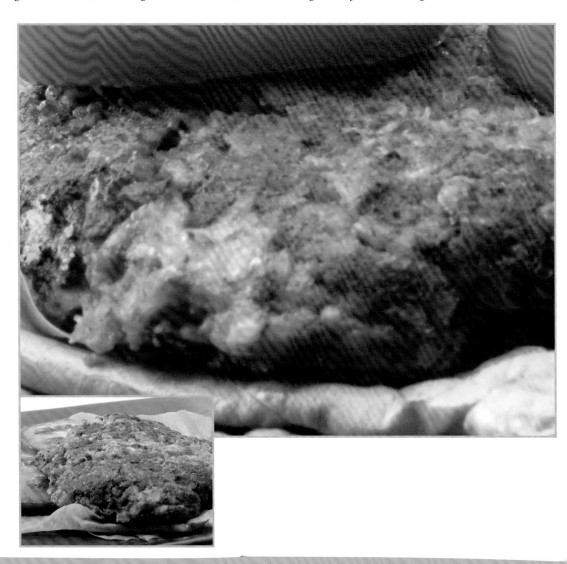

Black Bean Quinoa Burger

1 ½ cups cooked black beans
1 chipotle chili in adobo sauce
1 onion, chopped fine
6 cloves garlic, minced
2 T tomato paste
¼ tsp crushed red pepper
½ tsp chili powder
¾ tsp salt
½ tsp ground pepper
1 cup cooked quinoa
½ cup panko breadcrumbs
¼ cup cilantro, minced
½ cup Monterey Jack cheese, shredded
2 eggs (or 4 egg whites)
3 T walnut oil, divided

DIRECTIONS:

1. Place ½ cup of black beans in the bowl of the food processor with the chipotle chili. Pulse until well combined. Combine with remainder of black beans in a large bowl.

2. Heat skillet sprayed with olive oil spray over medium heat. Add onion and cook for 10 minutes. Stir in garlic, tomato paste, crushed red pepper, chili powder, salt and pepper and cook for one more minute. Remove from heat and combine with black bean mixture.

3. Add in quinoa, breadcrumbs and cilantro. Allow to cool for 3–4 minutes and add in eggs and cheese. For best results, place in refrigerator for one hour.

4. Form patties and place in the freezer for 10 minutes. Heat half of the walnut oil in a large skillet over medium heat. Cook for 3 minutes per side.

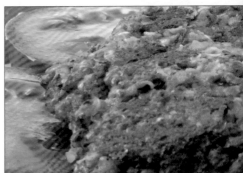

Make it Vegan: In place of eggs, use 2 T ground flax seeds mixed with 6 T water. Use ¼ cup mashed avocado and 1 T nutritional yeast in place of the cheese.

Make it Gluten-Free: Use gluten-free breadcrumbs.

Make it Cleaner: Use olive oil spray in place of the walnut oil.

Serving Size 77 g
Amount Per Serving Calories 188 Total Fat 8.2g Saturated Fat 3.6g Trans Fat 0.0g Cholesterol 62mg Sodium 354mg Total Carbohydrates 19.0g Dietary Fiber 3.7g Sugars 1.6g Protein 10.4g

I fell in love with Quinoa Patties when I tried Heidi Swanson's recipe in Super Natural Every Day. *Since then, I've tried making different variations to make the recipe more my own, and this is by far my favorite. If you are pressed for time, you can try starting with plain cooked quinoa. Here, however, I take advantage of how well quinoa absorbs flavors in cooking and cook the quinoa in vegetable broth with onion and garlic. If you don't have saffron threads on hand, feel free to omit.*

Blue Cheese Quinoa Patties

2 onions, chopped fine, divided
6 cloves garlic, minced
1 cup quinoa, rinsed
1 ½ cups vegetable broth
Pinch of saffron threads
3 T thyme or parsley (a mixture works great!)
¼ tsp crushed red pepper
1 tsp sea salt
½ tsp ground black pepper
5 eggs, beaten (or 10 egg whites)
1 T flour
4 oz good quality blue cheese
¾ cup breadcrumbs, preferably homemade and whole wheat
2 T extra-virgin olive oil

DIRECTIONS:

1. Spray a saucepan heated to medium with olive oil spray and add one onion. Cook for 10 minutes and add quinoa and garlic. Cook for 4 more minutes. Add in vegetable broth and bring to a simmer over medium-high. Reduce to low and simmer covered for 20 to 25 minutes. Stir in saffron, thyme, parsley, crushed red pepper, salt and black pepper and allow to sit covered for 5 minutes.

2. Allow quinoa to cool. Stir in eggs, blue cheese, flour and breadcrumbs. Allow to sit for a few minutes. Divide into 12 balls and squeeze each ball between your hands. Place the ball between your hands and flatten, shaping a small tight pattie.

3. Heat 2 T olive oil over medium-low. Place quinoa patties in the oil and press down. Cover and cook for 10 minutes. Flip and cook an additional 8 minutes.

Make it Vegan: Use vegan cheese and your favorite egg replacer. I like to use flax seeds as an egg replacer. Combine 5 T ground flax seeds with 15 T water. Allow to sit for 15 minutes until it develops a thick texture.

Make it Gluten-Free: Use gluten-free quinoa flour and make sure your breadcrumbs are gluten-free. To make your own, process gluten-free bread in your food processor and toss with a tablespoon of olive oil. Place in a skillet over medium high heat. Cook for 5 minutes, stirring frequently. Lower to medium low and cook another 8 minutes.

Serving Size 102 g
Amount Per Serving Total Fat 8.2g Saturated Fat 2.9g Trans Fat 0.0g Cholesterol 86mg Sodium 454mg Total Carbohydrates 17.5g Dietary Fiber 2.2g Sugars 1.5g Protein 8.2g

Don't let the long list of ingredients keep you from making this dish! It isn't nearly as time consuming to put together as you might think—as long as you let your food processor handle all of the heavy chopping. This creamy but low-fat sauce is a variation from most quinoa dishes, and is quite satisfying.

Broccoli Quinoa Salad

Herb Mixture
½ cup fresh parsley
⅓ cup fresh basil
1 T fresh dill
1 ½ tsp grated lemon rind
2 T fresh mint leaves
6 cloves garlic, peeled
Salad
6 cups broccoli, diced small
1 cup grape tomatoes, halved
2 cups cooked quinoa
2 shallots, minced
3 T capers
½ tsp pepper
14 oz artichoke hearts, drained and chopped
Dressing
3 T herb mixture
⅓ cup low-fat cottage cheese
¼ cup low-fat buttermilk
1 T fresh lemon juice
1 T red wine vinegar
1 T balsamic vinegar
1 T olive oil
1 T Dijon mustard
3 oz crumbled feta

DIRECTIONS:

1. Combine ingredients for herb mixture in the bowl of a food processor and pulse until well combined. Set aside 3 T for the dressing and reserve the remainder.

2. In a large bowl, combine broccoli, grape tomatoes, quinoa, shallots, capers and artichoke hearts. Top with reserved herb mixture.

3. Make Dressing: In the bowl of your food processor, place 3 T herb mixture, cottage cheese, buttermilk, lemon juice, vinegars, Dijon mustard, and olive oil. Process until well combined. Stir in feta and toss with broccoli mixture.

4. Chill for 30 minutes and serve.

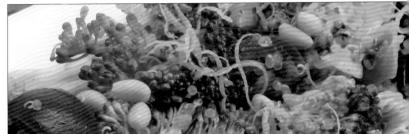

Make it Quick: Skip the fresh herbs and use dried as well as pre-chopped garlic. Alternatively, use a food processor to handle the chopping. You can buy pre-chopped broccoli and make the dressing one day ahead.

Make it Vegan: Skip the cottage cheese and buttermilk and instead use cashew cream. To make it, soak 2 cups of raw cashews overnight. Rinse and place in a blender with water to cover. Process until very fine. It will take a powerful 1000-watt blender to get cashews smooth. If yours doesn't do the job, simply strain off any lumpy pieces with the same colander that you use for washing quinoa.

Make it Gluten-Free: Double check your Dijon mustard and use gluten-free cottage cheese.

Make it Cleaner: Use fat-free cottage cheese and buttermilk, or skip the creamy dressing altogether and instead use more vinegar. Use chia gel in place of the olive oil.

6 servings
Calories 220 Calories from Fat 67 Total Fat 7.4g Saturated Fat 2.9g Trans Fat 0.0g Cholesterol 14mg Sodium 476mg Total Carbohydrates 29.9g Dietary Fiber 8.2g Sugars 4.1g

This is a fruity twist on one of my favorite combinations—butternut squash and quinoa! If you would like a little more "kick," try adding ⅛ tsp of cayenne pepper to the dish! Or, if you are cooking for children who would be put off by the garlic, simply omit it.

Caribbean Quinoa & Squash

4 cups diced butternut squash
1 cup of cooked quinoa
2 T olive oil, divided
2 T orange juice
2 T white balsamic vinegar
3 cloves garlic, minced
½ tsp mineral salt
½ tsp fresh ground black pepper
½ tsp tumeric
¼ cup dried apricots
¼ cup dried cranberries
3 T chopped chives
2 T slivered almonds

DIRECTIONS:

1. Preheat oven to 375 degrees. Combine diced squash and 1 T of the olive oil. Roast squash for 45 minutes or until tender.

2. Make Dressing: In a small bowl, whisk together olive oil, orange juice, vinegar, garlic, salt, pepper and tumeric.

3. Combine squash, quinoa, apricots and cranberries. Toss with dressing.

Make it Quick: Purchase pre-diced squash. Cutting up squash can be really time consuming—and unless your knives are sharp, a real pain. Skip the hassle and pick up pre-diced butternut squash at your grocery store.

Make it Cleaner: Make sure that your dried fruit is unsweetened.

4 servings
Calories 206 Total Fat 9.3g Saturated Fat 1.2g Trans Fat 0.0g Cholesterol 0mg Sodium 242mg Total Carbohydrates 29.2g Dietary Fiber 4.8g Sugars 5.1g

I know that packaged veggie burgers are not good for me . . . but I must confess that I just love them. I've spent a lot of time trying to find ones that I could make at home sans all the preservatives. This is a variation of one of the recipes for the website and I like it even better than the original. My parents are very much NOT vegetarian and until I happened to cook this while at their house, neither of them had ever had a veggie burger. My Dad told my Mom she had to get the recipe and asked for seconds, so I guess it was a winner. Feel free to substitute any oil that you have on hand for the walnut oil—just pay attention to how hot you get your pan if you are using olive oil—because it doesn't do well with high heat. Also, if you make your own breadcrumbs like I do, those will work as well.

Chipotle Quinoa Burger

1 cup cooked green lentils
2 chipotle chilies in adobo sauce
1 red onion, chopped fine
4 cloves garlic, minced
2 T tomato paste
1 tsp ground cumin
½ tsp chili powder
¾ tsp salt
½ tsp ground pepper
¾ cup cooked quinoa
½ cup panko breadcrumbs
1 T parsley
½ cup Monterey Jack cheese, shredded
2 eggs (or 4 egg whites)
3 T walnut oil, divided

DIRECTIONS:

1. Place half of lentils in a food processor with chipotle chilies. Process until well combined. Combine processed lentil mixture with remaining ½ cup lentils in a large bowl.

2. Heat large skillet over medium-high heat and coat with olive oil spray. Cook onion for 8–10 minutes, until tender. Add garlic, tomato paste, cumin, chili powder, salt and pepper. Cook for one more minute. Remove from heat and add to the lentil mixture.

3. Add in quinoa, breadcrumbs and parsley. When mixture has cooled slightly add in Monterey Jack cheese and eggs.

4. Place in refrigerator for 1 hour.

5. Form into thin patties and place on parchment paper in the freezer for 10 minutes. (I cover them with plastic wrap.)

6. Heat half of walnut oil over medium heat. Sauté for 3 minutes, checking to make sure burgers are not getting too brown. Flip and sauté 2–3 more minutes. Repeat with remainder of burgers.

Make it Vegan: You can choose to use vegan cheese, or just skip the cheese and add extra quinoa or breadcrumbs. Use your favorite egg replacer. I like to use flax seeds. Use 1 part flax seeds to 3 parts filtered water. Stir together until it forms a gel. For each egg you are replacing use 1 tablespoon of flax seeds and 3 tablespoons of water.

Make it Gluten-Free: Use gluten-free tomato paste and breadcrumbs. You may also use gluten-free oatmeal or quinoa flakes in place of the breadcrumbs.

Make it Cleaner: Use olive oil spray in place of the walnut oil.

6 servings
Calories 245 Total Fat 11.1g Saturated Fat 4.7g Trans Fat 0.0g Cholesterol 84mg Sodium 560mg Total Carbohydrates 23.2g Dietary Fiber 7.7g Sugars 2.1g Protein 14.6g

I learned a lot from the book Raising the Salad Bar *and this recipe is a direct result of that. Adding in citrus zest and juice to salads adds a lot of zip without adding a lot of calories or fat. This adaptation is a family favorite now, and it is eaten within a day every time I make it!*

Citrus Quinoa with Watercress & Balsamic Walnuts

1 cup quinoa, rinsed
3 cups washed watercress, chopped
1 carrot, peeled and shredded
½ cup dried cranberries
Zest of 1 lime
Zest of 1 orange
Dressing
¼ cup fresh orange juice
Juice of 1 lime
½ large shallot, diced
2 cloves garlic, minced
1 tsp agave nectar
2 T white balsamic vinegar
2 T olive oil
½ tsp mineral salt
¼ tsp ground black pepper
Balsamic Walnuts
1 cup walnuts
1 T balsamic vinegar
3 T agave nectar

DIRECTIONS:

1. Combine rinsed quinoa and 1 ½ cups water or broth in a saucepan. Bring to a simmering boil over medium. Reduce to low, cover and cook for 25 minutes. Remove from heat and allow to sit for another 5 minutes. Cool slightly.

2. Make walnuts: Preheat oven to 350 degrees. Stir together vinegar and agave nectar in a small microwave-safe bowl. Heat on high in the microwave for one minute. Toss walnuts in vinegar mixture. Place on a baking sheet lined with parchment paper and bake for 10 minutes.

3. Combine watercress, carrot, cranberries and zest in a large bowl. When quinoa is slightly cool toss with watercress mixture.

4. Make dressing: Combine orange juice, lime juice, shallot, garlic, agave nectar and vinegar in a small bowl. Add in olive oil in a steady stream. Season with salt and pepper.

5. Toss quinoa mixture with desired amount of dressing and top with walnuts.

{ Make it Quick: If time is tight, start with 3 cups of cooked quinoa and use regular chopped walnuts in place of the balsamic walnuts. }

Calories 298 Total Fat 18.5g Saturated Fat 1.5g Trans Fat 0.0g Cholesterol 0mg Sodium 173mg Total Carbohydrates 26.4g Dietary Fiber 4.3g Sugars 5.3g Protein 9.4g

This is a recipe that I originally shared on the website that didn't have quinoa in it. It was a healthy adaptation of eggplant parmesan that skipped the frying and I was so excited that my (Italian) family didn't know the difference that I just had to share. This was before I knew how great quinoa was blended into other dishes. Here, it almost disappears, adding substance without interfering with the taste or texture of the dish. It's a bit of work, but so worth it for a special occasion.

Eggplant Parmesan

DIRECTIONS:

1. Preheat oven to 375 degrees.

2. To make eggplant, cut eggplant into ¼ inch slices. This will be slightly thinner than what you may be used to, but it prevents the eggplant from getting soggy. Place a layer of the eggplant in a large colander. Sprinkle with salt. Continue the layers with all of the eggplant. This is going to help remove the moisture from the eggplant, so make sure that you place it on a towel or over a bowl.

3. Make Sauce—Heat the oil over medium heat. Add the garlic and cook until fragrant, about 90 seconds. Add tomatoes and ½ tsp salt. Increase the heat to medium-high and cook for 25 minutes or until the tomatoes start to break down. You may need to add water—1 T at a time—if your sauce starts to get dry before your tomatoes break down. Decrease heat to medium and cook for another 10 minutes. The sauce should be thick and chunky. Too much liquid will make the final dish watery. Remove from the heat and stir in basil leaves. Season to taste with salt and pepper.

4. Bread Eggplant—Combine the 3 eggs and the water in a bowl. Combine the panko and ⅓ cup of parmesan cheese in a separate dish. Dip the eggplant in the egg mixture and dredge in the breadcrumb mixture. You will want to lightly press the breadcrumbs so that they adhere. Place the eggplant on a baking sheet that has been lightly brushed with olive oil. Bake at 375 for 30 minutes, turning after 15 minutes.

5. Make filling by combining parmesan and next 5 ingredients.

6. To assemble, place ½ cup pasta sauce in the bottom of a 13 x 9 baking dish. Layer half of the eggplant slices and sprinkle with ⅛ teaspoon of salt. Top with ¾ cup pasta sauce, half of ricotta, ⅓ of mozzarella and ¼ cup parmesan cheese. Repeat layers once and end with remaining sauce. Cover and bake at 375 for 35 minutes. Uncover and add remaining mozzarella and remaining parmesan. Bake for an additional 10 minutes. Allow to cool for 10 to 15 minutes prior to serving.

To Make Eggplant
4 large eggs, lightly beaten
3 T water
2 ½–3 cups whole wheat panko breadcrumbs
⅓ cup parmesan cheese
3 eggplants, peeled and cut into ¼ inch slices
Olive oil
Filling
1 oz fresh parmesan
½ tsp crushed red pepper
2 cloves minced garlic
16 oz part-skim ricotta cheese
1 cup cooked quinoa
1 egg, lightly beaten
Sauce
3 T extra-virgin olive oil
½ tsp sea salt
4 large cloves of garlic, peeled and cut in half
2 28-oz cans of diced tomatoes
12 basil leaves, chopped
Remaining Ingredients
¼ tsp salt
8 oz fresh mozzarella cheese
¾ cup fresh parmesan cheese

Make it Gluten-Free: Be sure to use gluten-free breadcrumbs!

Make it Cleaner: Use skim ricotta and reduce all cheeses by half.

Make it Vegan: Use vegan cheese and your favorite egg replacer. I like to use flax seeds as an egg replacer. Combine 5 T ground flax seeds with 15 T water. Allow to sit for 15 minutes until it develops a thick texture. You could also use cashew cream in place of the ricotta cheese. Soak 2 cups raw whole cashews overnight in water. Drain and rinse. Place in a blender and cover with water. Process until smooth. If you don't have a high speed blender, strain nuts before proceeding.

Serving Size 394 g
Amount Per Serving Calories 390 Calories from Fat 167 Total Fat 18.6g Saturated Fat 7.9g Cholesterol 118mg Sodium 653mg Total Carbohydrates 35.6g Dietary Fiber 7.6g Sugars 8.6g Protein 22.4g

Lentil, Chickpea & Quinoa Burger with Cilantro Garlic Cream

¾ cup green lentils
Olive oil spray
1 onion, chopped fine
¾ cup cooked quinoa
1 ½ cup cooked chickpeas
1 egg
¼ cup chopped parsley
3 T chopped cilantro
2 cups breadcrumbs
½ tsp mineral salt
1 tsp thyme
½ tsp garlic powder
1 tsp sesame seeds
1 T olive oil
Cilantro Garlic Cream
1 cup nonfat Greek yogurt
2 cloves garlic, minced
2 T chopped cilantro
2 T chopped parsley

DIRECTIONS:

1. Heat 1 ½ cups of water to a boil. Add lentils and cook for 30 minutes or until tender. Meanwhile, heat olive oil spray and a pan over medium heat. Add onion and cook for 8 minutes.

2. Put chickpeas, quinoa, half of lentils, egg and onion into a food processor and process until smooth.

3. In a medium bowl, combine parsley, cilantro, breadcrumbs, remaining half of lentils and seasonings. Add chickpea mixture and stir until well combined.

4. Form into patties and refrigerate for 30 minutes and up to one hour.

5. Meanwhile, make Cilantro Garlic Cream by combining yogurt, garlic, cilantro and parsley. Refrigerate until ready to use.

6. Preheat olive oil in a skillet over medium heat. Add burgers and cook for 8 minutes on each side, or until golden brown.

7. Top with Cilantro Garlic Cream and serve!

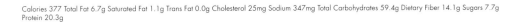

Make it Vegan: In place of egg, mix together 1 T ground flax seeds with 3 T water. For cream sauce, soak 1 cup cashews in water over night. Drain and rinse. Place in blender and add water to cover. Add in garlic, cilantro and parsley. Process until smooth.

Calories 377 Total Fat 6.7g Saturated Fat 1.1g Trans Fat 0.0g Cholesterol 25mg Sodium 347mg Total Carbohydrates 59.4g Dietary Fiber 14.1g Sugars 7.7g Protein 20.3g

There are few things that I enjoy more than a good quinoa salad. There is something about the simplicity and textures that always makes me feel nurtured. Feel free to experiment with this one! I think banana peppers would be a great addition, and if you are in the mood for a little cheese, feta would be perfect. Best of all? It will be just as good for lunch the next day!

Mediterranean Quinoa Salad

1 ½ tsp lemon rind, grated

3 T fresh lemon juice

2 T extra-virgin olive oil

1 tsp Dijon mustard

4 cloves garlic, minced

1 tsp fine mineral sea salt

½ tsp fresh ground pepper

2 cups cooked quinoa

¼ cup chopped fresh parsley

¼ cup red onion, chopped

½ cup chopped red pepper

¼ cup kalamata olives, chopped

1 (15-oz) can cannellini beans, rinsed and drained

DIRECTIONS:

1. In a small bowl, combine lemon rind, lemon juice, olive oil, Dijon mustard, garlic, salt and pepper.

2. In a large bowl, toss cooked quinoa, fresh parsley, onion and red pepper. Gently stir in cannellini beans and olives, being careful not to mash beans. Toss with dressing and chill for 30 minutes prior to serving.

Make it Cleaner: Skip the olive oil in the dressing and instead use chia gel. To make it, combine ⅓ cup chia seeds with 2 cups of water. Pulse in your blender and allow to sit for 20 minutes, pulsing every 5 minutes or so. Store for up to a week in the refrigerator and use 1:1 as a replacement for all or part of the olive oil in any salad dressing recipe you choose.

6 servings
Calories 327 Total Fat 6.8g Saturated Fat 0.9g Trans Fat 0.0g Cholesterol 0mg Sodium 388mg Total Carbohydrates 51.2g Dietary Fiber 17.2g Sugars 2.2g Protein 17.4g

I wish I could say that the idea of making Mexican rice by cooking it in the oven in pureed tomatoes and onion was my idea, but the credit goes to Cooks Illustrated. I've made my Mexican rice like this for a while and one day I started to wonder what I would need to do to prepare quinoa in just the same manner. The answer was a definite—yes, you can prepare quinoa in the oven! I surprised myself with this one because this is not the type of dish I go nuts for, but when I made this I couldn't stop eating it. It is intended as a side dish, but add a little cheese on top and you have a meal. I will admit that the photos aren't the best, but please don't let that stop you. This is also a great starter for any Mexican quinoa salad or soup.

Oven Mexican Quinoa

2 large tomatoes, cored and quartered

1 red onion, sliced into 8 pieces

3 jalapeños, seeded and cored and diced, divided

6 cloves garlic

1/4 cup walnut oil

2 cups rinsed quinoa

2 cups vegetable broth

1 tsp mineral sea salt

1 tsp cumin

1 T tomato paste

1/2 cup fresh cilantro, chopped

Juice of 1 lime

DIRECTIONS:

1. Preheat oven to 350 degrees. In your food processor, combine tomatoes, red onion, 2 jalapeños and garlic. Pulse until well combined. You should have about 2 cups.

2. Heat walnut oil over medium heat in an oven-safe skillet. Add quinoa and cook for 5–8 minutes, stirring often. Add jalapeño and cook 1 more minute. Add in vegetable broth, salt, cumin and tomato paste.

3. Cover with an oven-safe lid or tightly with foil and bake for 35 minutes, carefully stirring every 15 minutes. Add in cilantro and lime and enjoy!

Make it Cleaner: Skip the walnut oil and use a bit of olive oil spray. Cook for 2–3 minutes, stirring constantly, before proceeding.

Make it Gluten-Free: Ensure that the broth and tomato paste are vegan.

Make it Quick: Purchase a tube of cilantro to avoid chopping and use minced pickled jalapeños. You could also use 2 cups of salsa in place of the tomatoes/onion/jalapeño and garlic mixture.

8 servings
Calories 205 Total Fat 5.3g Saturated Fat 0.5g Cholesterol 0mg Sodium 433mg Total Carbohydrates 31.8g Dietary Fiber 4.4g Sugars 2.6g Protein 8.8g

I was born in Georgia, so I suppose it's natural that I love peaches! Up until recently, I'd never tried them with quinoa before! The combination of peaches and red pepper creates a dish that is slightly sweet, but savory enough for a main course.

Peach & Walnut Salad

1 cup quinoa (or 3 cups of cooked quinoa)
1 cup parsley, finely chopped
½ cup walnuts, chopped
2 peaches, peeled and diced
½ red bell pepper, diced
1 T extra-virgin olive oil
2 T lime juice
2 T red wine vinegar
⅓ cup orange juice
2 cloves garlic, minced
½ tsp chili powder
½ tsp mineral sea salt
½ tsp fresh ground black pepper
¼ cup feta (low-fat is ok)

DIRECTIONS:

1. Combine quinoa and water and bring to a boil. Boil uncovered for 10 minutes. Remove from heat and drain in a fine metal strainer. Rinse with cool water. Bring 2 inches of water to a boil. Place quinoa over water in the strainer and cover. Steam for 10 minutes. Remove from heat and carefully uncover, being sure to avoid burning yourself on the steam.

2. Toss quinoa with parsley, walnuts, peaches and pepper.

3. In a small bowl, blend oil, lime juice, red wine vinegar, orange juice, garlic, chili powder, pepper and salt. Toss with quinoa mixture. Top with crumbled feta and drizzle with more red wine vinegar, if desired.

Make it Quick: Start with cooked quinoa. Buy pre-cut parsley that comes in tubes if you are really short on time.

Make it Vegan: Skip the cheese and add an extra ¼ cup walnuts.

Make it Cleaner: Opt for low fat cheese and omit the olive oil, if you want.

Make it Gluten-Free: This dish is naturally gluten-free!

Serving Size 191 g
Calories 350 Total Fat 17.5g Saturated Fat 2.6g Trans Fat 0.0g Cholesterol 5mg Sodium 447mg Total Carbohydrates 37.4g Dietary Fiber 5.7g Sugars 7.0g

Poblano chilies are very mild and are often used for stuffing. Here, I've roasted them and then created a puree which seasons the quinoa as it cooks. Top it off with just a bit of either cheddar or pepper jack cheese and you've got a meal that is satisfying without a lot of extra calories. For a pretty presentation, serve in a red bell pepper!

Poblano Chili Quinoa

1 cup quinoa

1 ½ cups vegetable broth

4 poblano chilies

1 red pepper, diced

½ red onion, diced

4 tsp garlic, minced

1 cup corn, thawed

½ cup shredded cheddar or pepper jack cheese

DIRECTIONS:

1. Adjust top rack in the oven to be 2–3 inches from the broiler. Preheat oven to broil. Place poblano chilies on the top rack and broil until black, turning as needed.

2. Place in paper bag and allow to steam for 15 minutes. Peel, seed and chop. Puree until smooth.

3. Spray olive oil in a large saucepan. Add onion and pepper and cook for 10 minutes. Add garlic and chili puree and cook for another minute. Add quinoa and vegetable broth and bring to a simmer. Reduce to low, cover and cook for 20 minutes.

4. Add corn and cheese and stir until cheese is melted, about 5 more minutes.

5. Top with additional cheese if desired and serve warm.

Make it Vegan: Either use vegan cheese or skip the cheese altogether and instead top with some spicy toasted almonds.

Make it Cleaner: Opt for low-fat cheese or skip the cheese.

Make it Gluten-Free: Make sure your vegetable broth doesn't have any hidden gluten.

Make it Quick: Prepare the peppers a day ahead, and opt for pre-cut peppers and onions.

4 servings
Serving Size 274 g Calories 256 Total Fat 4.6g Saturated Fat 1.1g Cholesterol 3mg Sodium 386mg Total Carbohydrates 41.9g Dietary Fiber 5.4g Sugars 5.7g Protein 13.7g

Though I really enjoy falafel, my husband is not a fan. The reason? Most falafel recipes are way too dry! The addition of quinoa here adds both moisture and a good nutritional boost.

Quinoa Falafel

2 cups cooked chickpeas (about 1 can)
2 T tahini
1 cup cooked quinoa
1 tsp sea salt
1 tsp baking powder
1 tsp ground cumin
2 T fresh cilantro, chopped
½ tsp cayenne pepper
4 cloves garlic, minced
Juice of 1 lemon
2 T olive oil
1 cup arugula
½ cup Greek yogurt
4 cloves garlic, minced

DIRECTIONS:

1. Preheat oven to 375 degrees.

2. In a food processor, combine chickpeas, tahini, quinoa, salt, baking powder, cumin, cilantro, cayenne pepper, garlic and lemon. Pulse until well combined. Form into 18 balls and then flatten into patties.

3. Heat olive oil in an oven-safe skillet over medium heat. Add patties and cook for 5 minutes on each side, until lightly browned. Place skillet in the oven and bake for 15 minutes.

4. Make sauce by combining Greek yogurt and garlic.

5. Place falafel on top of arugula and top with yogurt.

Make it Vegan: Simply allow vegan yogurt to strain in cheesecloth overnight in the refrigerator and you will have a thicker Greek-like yogurt.

4 servings
Serving Size 198g Calories 307 Total Fat 13.4g Saturated Fat 2.0g Cholesterol 1mg Sodium 243mg Total Carbohydrates 36.7g Dietary Fiber 2.0g Sugars 7.4g

This is a great salad to make when you are craving a caprese salad, but the tomatoes aren't quite in season yet. I find that grape tomatoes are far more forgiving. The balsamic reduction is optional, but really gives it that gourmet kick! To make the balsamic reduction you will want to put the vinegar in a saucepan over high heat. Whisk constantly to avoid burning. Bring to a boil and add in a teaspoon of agave nectar or sugar if desired. Turn down the heat and simmer until it is reduced by at least half—more if you want thicker syrup. If you don't want to take the time to make the reduction, you can always buy reduced vinegar or just add a splash of regular balsamic vinegar, which will not be as sweet and will add a little more bite to the dish.

Quinoa Salad Caprese

2 cups cooked quinoa

1 cup diced fresh mozzarella cheese

½ cup grape tomatoes, cut in half

1 T olive oil

2 T balsamic vinegar

2 T fresh basil, chopped

½ tsp oregano

1 tsp of fresh cracked pepper

4 cloves garlic, minced

Balsamic Reduction, for drizzling (optional)

DIRECTIONS:

1. In a medium bowl, combine cooked quinoa, mozzarella cheese and tomatoes.

2. In a small bowl, combine olive oil, balsamic vinegar, basil, oregano, pepper and garlic.

3. Toss dressing with quinoa mixture. Salt and pepper to taste and drizzle with balsamic reduction if desired.

{ Make it Vegan: Substitute any vegan cheese or use pine nuts in place of the cheese and add a touch of nutritional yeast. }

Serves 4
Serving Size 89 g Amount Per Serving Calories 224 Total Fat 10.7g Saturated Fat 4.3g Trans Fat 0.0g Cholesterol 15mg Sodium 152mg Total Carbohydrates 20.1g Dietary Fiber 2.3g Sugars 0.7g Protein 11.5g

I must admit that I was surprised at how well this dish was received. I knew I would like it, but my family loved it as well. I actually started out with about half the vegetables and then liked them so much I went back and made another batch. Feel free to switch up the vegetables depending on what you can find. This is a fun dish to play around with.

Quinoa Salad with Roasted Vegetables

2 cups quinoa, rinsed
3 cups of vegetable broth
2 heads of garlic, broken into cloves
2 zucchinis, diced
2 carrots, diced
2 red onions, sliced small
2 red peppers, diced
¼ cup extra-virgin olive oil
Mineral sea salt
Fresh ground black pepper
1 T tomato paste
¼ cup lemon juice
4 cloves garlic, minced
⅛ cup crushed red pepper
2 T olive oil
2 T balsamic vinegar
½ cucumber, peeled, seeded and cut into ¼ inch dice
3 oz feta cheese, crumbled (optional)

DIRECTIONS:

1. Preheat the oven to 400 degrees

2. In a saucepan, mix quinoa and vegetable broth. Bring to a boil. Reduce heat to medium-low and simmer covered for 15 minutes. Remove from heat and allow to remain covered.

3. Toss garlic with 1 T of the olive oil. Salt and pepper to taste and place in a small dish. Cover with foil.

4. Meanwhile, place zucchinis, carrots, onions and peppers on a large baking sheet. Drizzle with all but 2 T of the remaining olive oil and season with salt and pepper. Toss carefully. Add to the oven along with the garlic and roast for 45 minutes.

5. Remove vegetables and garlic from oven and allow to cool.

6. Toss quinoa with tomato paste and fold in the roasted vegetables. Squeeze garlic from cloves and add to the quinoa and vegetables.

7. In a small dish, combine remaining 2 T of olive oil, lemon juice, minced garlic and crushed red pepper. Season with mineral salt and ground black pepper. Toss with quinoa and cooled vegetables.

8. Serve at room temperature or chilled.

Make it Gluten-Free: Ensure that you are using gluten-free tomato paste.

Make it Cleaner: Skip the cheese and omit the oil in the dressing. Use chia gel if desired.

Make it Vegan: Use vegan cheese or top with toasted pine nuts and a sprinkle of nutritional yeast.

Make it Quick: With roasting vegetables, there is really not a quick solution. Start with cooked quinoa. Roast and peel the garlic and chop the vegetables a day ahead of time.

Serves 6
Serving Size 316 g Calories 341 Total Fat 15.9g Saturated Fat 3.5g Trans Fat 0.0g Cholesterol 9mg Sodium 430mg Total Carbohydrates 39.9g Dietary Fiber 5.7g Sugars 5.7g Protein 11.4g

This recipe was inspired by a Cooking Light recipe that originally didn't use quinoa at all! It is simple to make, but beautiful and tasty enough for company.

Quinoa Stuffed Butternut Squash

2 butternut squash
1 T olive oil
2 red bell peppers, seeded and diced
½ cup green onions, sliced
2 cups vegetable broth
1 cup quinoa, rinsed
1 tsp sage
2 T fresh parsley, chopped
2 oz Gruyère cheese

DIRECTIONS:

1. Preheat oven to 350 degrees. Cut squash in half lengthwise and use a spoon to scoop the seeds and membranes out. Spray a large baking sheet with olive oil spray and place squash facedown. Bake for 35 minutes. Allow to cool slightly and then scoop out pulp, leaving a ¼-inch shell. Mash scooped-out pulp with a fork.

2. Meanwhile, heat olive oil in a medium saucepan. Add diced red peppers and green onions and sauté for 6 minutes. Add vegetable broth, quinoa and sage and bring to a boil. Reduce heat to medium-low. Cover and simmer for 15 minutes. Stir in parsley and allow to sit covered for 5 more minutes. Salt and pepper to taste.

3. Mix mashed butternut squash with quinoa mixture and place in shell.

4. Top with Gruyere cheese and place under the broiler for 5 minutes or until cheese is melted.

A Gluten-Free Dish

Make it Cleaner: Use olive oil spray instead of olive oil and low-fat cheese

Make it Vegan: Use vegan cheese or top with walnuts in the last 15 minutes of baking.

Make it Quick: Used precooked quinoa and simply mix with the peppers and green onions after they have cooked. Stir in parsley and sage.

Serves 8
Serving Size 239 g Calories 190 Total Fat 5.8g Saturated Fat 1.9g Cholesterol 8mg Sodium 223mg Total Carbohydrates 28.7g Dietary Fiber 4.5g Sugars 4.1g

This is a light dish that is perfect as a side dish but can also be used as a main course. If you don't have white balsamic vinegar, you can substitute regular. Your results will still be great.

Quinoa with Apples, Cranberries & Pine Nuts

2 T extra-virgin olive oil
1 ½ cups quinoa, rinsed
1 onion, diced
1 tsp dried thyme
2 cups vegetable broth
2 oz pine nuts
¼ cup extra-virgin olive oil
3 T white balsamic vinegar
1 tsp minced garlic
1 shallot, minced
1 tart apple
½ cup dried cranberries
½ cup parsley, finely chopped
Goat cheese (optional)

DIRECTIONS:

1. Heat 2 T olive oil in a large saucepan over moderate heat. Add onion and thyme and cook for 5 minutes over low heat, stirring frequently. Add quinoa and cook for 2 to 3 minutes, until lightly toasted. Add vegetable broth and 1 tsp mineral salt. Bring to a simmer. Reduce to low and cook covered for 25 minutes. Remove from heat and allow to remain covered for 5 minutes.

2. Meanwhile, preheat oven to 350 degrees. Place pine nuts in a small pan and roast until golden, about 5 minutes. Allow to cool. (Tip: if you can't find pine nuts or they are too pricey, use toasted walnuts, almonds or cashews.)

3. In a small bowl, whisk together olive oil, vinegar, shallot, and garlic. Season to taste with salt and pepper.

4. Combine quinoa, apple, cranberries and parsley. Toss with dressing. Top with pine nuts just prior to serving.

5. Top with goat cheese if desired.

Make it Gluten-Free: Ensure that broth chosen is gluten-free.

Make it Cleaner: Use 2 T olive oil instead of ¼ cup. Omit the goat cheese.

Make it Vegan: Omit the goat cheese or choose vegan cheese.

Make it Quick: Cook onion and thyme and stir in cooked quinoa.

Serves 8
Serving Size 160 g Amount Per Serving Calories 281 Calories from Fat 155 Total Fat 17.2g Saturated Fat 2.1g Trans Fat 0.0g Cholesterol 0mg Sodium 196mg Total Carbohydrates 26.0g Dietary Fiber 3.6g Sugars 3.6g Protein 6.8g

This is a simple recipe that can be made regardless of your skill level in the kitchen. I love all the colors and the slight bite that the vinegar gives the dish. For a special touch when I'm having this as a main course, I like to top it with goat cheese. Any soft cheese would work!

Quinoa with Roasted Butternut Squash & Cranberries

12 oz butternut squash, diced
1 red onion, diced
1 T chopped fresh sage
1 T chopped fresh thyme
3 T olive oil, divided
2 cups cooked quinoa
1 ½ T balsamic vinegar
4 cloves garlic, minced
½ cup dried cranberries
½ cup chopped pecans

DIRECTIONS:

1. Preheat oven to 375 degrees. Toss squash, onion, sage and thyme with 2 T olive oil. Season to taste with salt and pepper. Roast for 45 minutes.

2. Warm cooked quinoa and combine with cranberries and pecans

3. Toss balsamic vinegar, 1 T olive oil and garlic in a small bowl. Combine squash and quinoa mixture and toss with dressing.

Make it Quick: If you are short on time you can buy frozen diced butternut squash that can be cooked in a fraction of the time it takes to cook fresh squash. Start with cooked quinoa and you can have this dish together in no time!

Serves 6
Serving Size 123 g Calories 230 Total Fat 14.5g Saturated Fat 1.7g Trans Fat 0.0g Cholesterol 0mg Sodium 5mg Total Carbohydrates 23.1g Dietary Fiber 4.2g Sugars 2.8g Protein 4.3g

Don't let the fact that this dish is so, well, GREEN scare you. I promise, it tastes nothing like a green smoothie. (And I like green smoothies, but I'm just saying . . . this is really tasty!) Play around with the greens and use what you have on hand—it would be good with just spinach or kale. If you prefer, you could also substitute the pecans with pine nuts!

Quinoa with Spinach Kale Pecan Pesto

1 T olive oil
1 onion, chopped
1 red pepper, chopped
3 carrots, peeled and cut diagonally
1 ½ cups quinoa
3 cups vegetable broth
6 oz kale, stems removed and torn into pieces
6 oz baby spinach
¼ cup pecans, toasted
8 cloves garlic, peeled
½ cup grated parmesan
¼ cup olive oil
2 T balsamic vinegar
½ tsp mineral salt
¼ tsp cayenne pepper
½ tsp black pepper

DIRECTIONS:

1. Heat olive oil over medium heat. Add onion and red pepper and cook until tender, about 8 minutes. Add in carrots and cook for 2 minutes. Add quinoa and 3 cups of vegetable broth. Bring to a simmer and then reduce heat to low. Cover and cook for 25 minutes. Allow to remain covered for an additional 5 minutes.

2. Meanwhile, place kale and spinach in a large pot with boiling water. Cover and heat over medium-high heat. Cook for 5 minutes or until kale is still bright green but wilted. Drain and reserve cooking liquid. Allow kale to cool.

3. Chop together pecans and garlic in a food processor. Add in kale and spinach and blend completely. Add in parmesan (kale and spinach should be completely cooled first) and blend. Add oil and vinegar. If needed, add in cooking liquid until desired consistency has been reached. Season with salt and pepper.

4. Combine quinoa mixture with pesto and toss. Serve warm, topping with additional parmesan if desired.

Make it Cleaner: If you are really trying to watch your oil, you could reduce the olive oil to ⅛ cup, but you will need to add in a little broth or chia gel so that you can achieve a smooth consistency.

Make it Quick: Start with cooked quinoa and prepare the pesto up to a day ahead of time.

Serves 8
Serving Size 239 g Calories 291 Total Fat 15.3g Saturated Fat 2.9g Trans Fat 0.0g Cholesterol 6mg Sodium 525mg Total Carbohydrates 28.7g Dietary Fiber 4.6g Sugars 2.9g Protein 10.8g

I made this dish when the collard greens from my Dad's garden came in! Although I'm not typically one to enjoy dishes like these, it was a big hit around our house. My Dad, who isn't crazy about garbanzo beans, was even hunting down the leftovers for lunch the next day. You need to pay attention to the size of your crock pot and you may need to adjust the amounts. Mine is one of the largest capacities that you can get and it was very full!

Slow Cooker Curried Chickpeas & Quinoa

2 ¼ cups dried chickpeas, rinsed and soaked overnight
1 rutabaga, peeled and cut into ¾-inch dices
1 onion, finely chopped
5 cloves garlic, chopped
1 bay leaf
5 tsp curry powder
2 tsp chili powder
1 lb collard greens, stems removed and chopped
1 ¼ tsp sea salt, divided
Fresh ground black pepper
1 ½ cups quinoa, rinsed
¾ cup roasted red peppers, diced
1 cup nonfat Greek yogurt
4 cloves garlic, minced
1 jalapeño, minced
¼ cup chopped cilantro
Juice of 1 lime

DIRECTIONS:

1. Rinse soaked chickpeas and combine with rutabaga, onion, quinoa, garlic and bay leaf in slow cooker. Add 5 cups of water and cook on low for 8–10 hours or high for 4–5 hours. Add in curry and chili powders in the last 30 minutes of cooking.

2. Stir and add in half of collards. Cover and allow to cook for 5 minutes, until collards are wilted. Add remainder of greens and cook for remaining time. Season with salt and pepper.

3. In a small bowl, mix greek yogurt, garlic, jalapeño, cilantro and lime juice. Ladle chickpea/quinoa mixture into bowl. Top with roasted red peppers and a dollop of yogurt mixture.

{ Make it Vegan: Use a non-dairy yogurt for the sauce. Alternately, you could use cashew cream as the base of the sauce. }

Serving Size 172 g
Amount Per Serving Calories 258 Total Fat 3.7g Trans Fat 0.0g Cholesterol 1mg Sodium 255mg Total Carbohydrates 44.2g Dietary Fiber 10.8g Sugars 7.4g Protein 13.9g

This quinoa salad is perfect in the late spring and summer when vegetables are at their best. Light and healthy, this is a real crowd-pleaser. If you are in the mood for pasta, try substituting quinoa pasta in place of the quinoa.

Summer Quinoa Salad

DIRECTIONS:

1. In a large bowl, combine quinoa, peppers, red onion, grape tomatoes, olives and artichoke hearts.

2. In a small bowl, make dressing by combining garlic, vinegar, Italian seasoning, salt and pepper. Add in olive oil and combine until emulsified. Toss with quinoa mixture and top with fresh basil.

3 cups cooked quinoa
1 each yellow, green and red bell pepper, cored and sliced in strips
1 red onion, sliced thin
1 cup grape tomatoes, sliced in half
2/3 cup kalamata olives, pitted and sliced in half
14 oz artichoke hearts
6 cloves garlic
1/4 cup balsamic vinegar
1/4 cup red wine vinegar
1/4 cup extra-virgin olive oil
1 tsp Italian seasoning
1 tsp mineral sea salt
1/2 tsp pepper
1 cup basil leaves, chopped thin

Make it Quick: Purchase olives that are already pitted and sliced, and instead of the vegetables listed here choose whatever vegetables that you can find pre-sliced at your grocery store. You could also choose to make it with a purchased vinaigrette dressing, or just use whatever homemade dressing that you have on hand!

Make it Cleaner: Skip the olive oil in the dressing and instead use chia gel. Remember chia pets? Well, these seeds now have a whole new role . . . in your kitchen. Chia seeds are loaded with essential fatty acids, antioxidants and phytonutrients. They slow the absorption of carbohydrates into the blood stream and chia gel makes a great substitution of olive oil in salad dressings. To make it, combine 1/3 cup chia seeds with 2 cups of water. Pulse in your blender and allow to sit for 20 minutes, pulsing every 5 minutes or so. Store for up to a week in the refrigerator and use 1:1 as a replacement for all or part of the olive oil in any salad dressing recipe you choose.

Make it Gluten-Free: Olives and artichoke hearts are typically gluten-free, but its always a good idea to double check.

Serves 4
Serving Size 362 g Calories 305 Total Fat 17.6g Saturated Fat 2.4g Trans Fat 0.0g Cholesterol 1mg Sodium 767mg Total Carbohydrates 32.8g Dietary Fiber 9.7g Sugars 5.4g Protein 7.5g

With all its creamy richness, this dish is just a little bit indulgent, but oh so worth it. I love the heat from the chipotle pepper! All of the flavors combine to make this a dish worthy of a special occasion

Sweet Potato, Quinoa & Butternut Squash Gratin

2 T olive oil
1 large shallot, minced
4 cloves garlic, minced
1 chipotle chili in adobo sauce
1 T adobo sauce
2 garlic cloves, minced
5 T quinoa flour
½ tsp dried thyme
2 cups low fat-milk
¾ cup parmesan cheese
½ tsp salt
½ tsp freshly ground black pepper
3 cups sweet potato, peeled and cut into cubes
½ large butternut squash, peeled and cut into cubes
1 ¾ cups cooked quinoa
½ cup shredded Gruyère cheese

DIRECTIONS:

1. Preheat oven to 350 degrees.

2. Heat olive oil over medium heat in a large saucepan. Add shallot, garlic, chipotle chili, garlic and adobo sauce and cook for 3 minutes. Add 4 T quinoa flour and thyme and cook for 2 more minutes, stirring constantly. Slowly stir in milk and whisk until well combined. Stir constantly for 3 minutes until mixture starts to thicken. Add parmesan cheese and cook until cheese melts. Remove from heat and salt and pepper to taste.

3. Bring a large pot of water to boil. Carefully placed diced sweet potatoes in pot and boil for 4 minutes. Remove with a slotted spoon. Add squash and boil for 4 minutes. Drain.

4. Spray olive oil in an 11 x 7 baking dish. Add potatoes, squash and cooked quinoa and stir to combine. Cover with sauce and top with Gruyère cheese.

5. Bake for 40 minutes. Preheat broiler and broil for an additional 3 minutes, until top is golden brown.

Make it Vegan: Use vegan cheese and the non-dairy milk of your choice. (I like unsweetened almond milk.)

Make it Cleaner: Use nonfat milk, low-fat parmesan and cut the Gruyère in half.

Make it Gluten-Free: Hooray! This dish is gluten-free!

Make it Quick: This dish can be made through step 4 up to 24 hours in advance. Place in the oven cold and preheat oven. Bake for 50 minutes.

Serves 8
Serving Size 218 g Amount Per Serving Calories 293 Total Fat 10.2g Saturated Fat 3.9g Trans Fat 0.0g Cholesterol 19mg Sodium 427mg Total Carbohydrates 39.4g Dietary Fiber 4.9g Sugars 5.4g Protein 11.8g

One of the things I missed most when I went vegetarian was my Mom's Chicken Pot Pie. It has always been the ultimate comfort food to me. I had long wondered how quinoa would do in a pot pie, but I hadn't tried it because I was afraid the texture would be all wrong. Boy am I glad I did! This is one dish that even carnivores won't miss the meat in (though chicken or turkey could certainly be added)! I'm funny about the textures of leftovers and was afraid that this wouldn't be good the next day, but actually it was almost as good as when it was first cooked.

Vegetable & Quinoa Pot Pie

1 potato, peeled and diced
1 red onion, chopped fine
2 carrots, peeled and sliced
1 cup frozen corn, thawed
1 cup frozen peas, thawed
2 cups cooked quinoa
3 T flour (I used quinoa flour)
3 ½ cups vegetable broth
½ cup milk
7 sheets phyllo dough

DIRECTIONS:

1. Preheat oven to 450 degrees. Place diced potato in a small pot of boiling water and boil until tender, about 5 minutes.

2. Meanwhile, heat olive oil spray over medium heat. Add onion and carrots and cook for 10 minutes, until tender.

3. In a medium bowl, combine flour, broth and milk. Add to onion mixture and simmer until slightly thickened, about 4 minutes. Add corn, peas and quinoa.

4. Spray a square baking dish with olive oil spray and add vegetable mixture. Top with phyllo dough, spraying each sheet as you add it with olive oil.

5. Bake for 25–35 minutes, until the crust is golden brown.

Make it Vegan: I'm not aware of commercially available vegan phyllo dough, but any vegan pie crust would work just as well as phyllo. Substitute the dairy-free milk of your choice.

Make it Quick: Use frozen mixed vegetables. You could also make the filling ahead of time and then top with phyllo when you are ready to pop it in the oven.

Make it Gluten-Free: Use a gluten-free pie crust. Ensure that your vegetable broth is gluten-free—some are and some aren't, so make sure you read the labels! Use the gluten-free flour of your choice.

Serves 6
Serving Size 324 g Amount Per Serving Calories 261 Total Fat 4.3g Saturated Fat 1.0g Trans Fat 0.0g Cholesterol 2mg Sodium 601mg Total Carbohydrates 44.7g Dietary Fiber 5.6g Sugars 5.6g Protein 11.2g

Just because I don't eat meat anymore does not mean that my cravings for Mexican foods have gone away! In fact—I think they are stronger than ever! This is an easy vegetarian burrito recipe which could also easily be adapted for meat eaters. Just reduce the quinoa by ¼ cup and add in ¾ cup of shredded chicken. This recipe is especially good when topped with guacamole!

Vegetarian Quinoa Burrito

DIRECTIONS:

1. Combine quinoa, lime juice, cayenne, cumin, garlic and 1½ cups water in a saucepan. Bring to a simmer and reduce heat to low. Cook covered for 25 to 30 minutes. Remove from heat. Stir in black beans and allow to sit covered for 5 more minutes.

2. Preheat oven to 400 degrees.

3. Add green onions, corn, lime zest, red peppers and cilantro to the quinoa mixture. Salt and pepper to taste.

4. Fill tortillas with quinoa mixture and place them seam side down in a baking dish. Top with cheese and cover with foil. Bake for 10 minutes. Remove foil and bake 15 minutes more.

5. Top with salsa and diced jalapeños and enjoy!

³/₄ cup quinoa, rinsed
4 tsp lime juice
¹/₈ tsp cayenne pepper
½ tsp cumin
4 cloves garlic, minced
1 cup cooked black beans
2 green onions
½ cup corn kernels (fresh or frozen)
Zest of one lime
¹/₄ cup roasted red peppers
2 T fresh cilantro
6 whole wheat or gluten-free tortillas
1 ½ cups vegan or regular cheddar cheese
½ cup salsa
Diced jarred jalapeños (optional)
Salt and pepper to taste

Make it Vegan: Instead of covering it with cheese, top it with salsa and diced avocados!

Serves 6
Amount Per Serving Calories 359 Total Fat 11.8g Cholesterol 30mg (with cheese) Sodium 517mg Total Carbohydrates 47.2g Dietary Fiber 7.4g Protein 16.9g

It goes without saying that this is NOT the healthiest dish in the book. But sometimes you just need a little comfort food and this certainly fits the bill, without the white carbs that come along with traditional macaroni and cheese. Also missing is the butter! What remains, however, is comfort food for those times when you really need it!

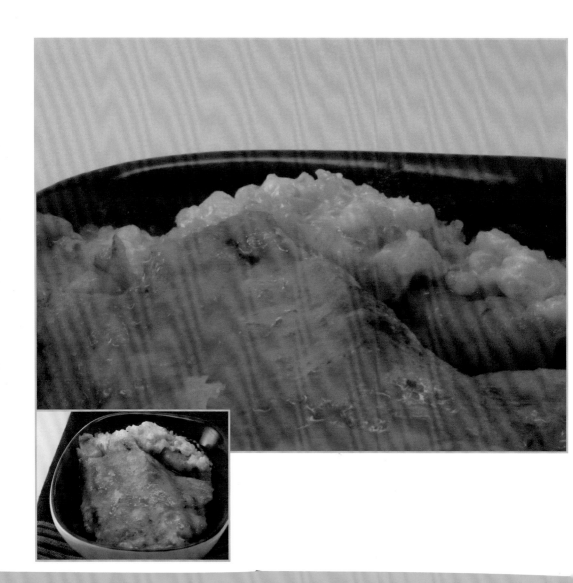

Yummy Quinoa & Cheese

DIRECTIONS:

1. Preheat broiler. In a large oven-proof skillet, bring 3 cups of water and 1 cup of the evaporated milk to a simmer over medium-high heat. Add quinoa and return to a simmering boil. Reduce to low. Cover and cook for 15 minutes, or until quinoa is tender.

2. In a small bowl, whisk together remaining evaporated milk, cornstarch and Dijon mustard. Add to quinoa and cook for another 2 minutes. Stir in Gruyère and Fontina by the handful until melted.

3. Top with cheddar cheese. Broil until golden brown, about 3 minutes. Allow to cool for 10–15 minutes before serving.

3 cups water
12 oz evaporated milk
2 cups quinoa, well rinsed
1 tsp cornstarch
1 T Dijon mustard
2 cups Gruyère cheese, shredded
2 cups Fontina cheese, shredded
1 cup cheddar, shredded

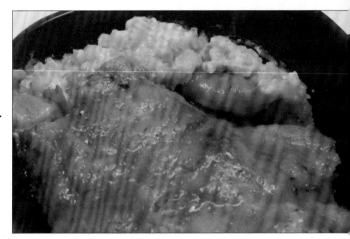

Make it Quick: This dish comes together really quickly, but you can make it even easier if you break out your food processor to grate your cheeses. I like to do this once a week, typically when I get home from the grocery store.

Make it Vegan: Use vegan cheeses and skip the evaporated milk and use cashew cream instead. To make it, soak 2 cups of raw cashews overnight. Rinse and place in a blender with water to cover. Process until very fine. It will take a powerful 1000-watt blender to get cashews smooth. If yours doesn't do the job, simply strain off any lumpy pieces with the same colander that you use for washing quinoa.

Make it Gluten-Free: Just make sure that you don't use processed cheeses and to check the label on your mustard to ensure that it is gluten-free.

Make it Cleaner: The whole point of this dish is to be a little bit indulgent. But, if you wanted to make it healthier, you could reduce the amount of cheese by half and use low-fat cheddar or skip the cheddar altogether.

8 servings
Serving Size 242 g Calories 448 Total Fat 23.8g Saturated Fat 13.1g Trans Fat 0.0g Cholesterol 76mg Sodium 465mg Total Carbohydrates 31.1g Dietary Fiber 2.9g Sugars 4.9g Protein 27.0g

Quinoa Pasta, Polenta & Pizza

While my youngest son loves spaghetti, I've never been all that crazy about it. Especially since becoming a vegetarian—it's always seemed like something was missing. This dish changed that! Everyone in my house really enjoyed this, to my utter amazement. I like all quinoa pasta, but, I will have to say that quinoa spaghetti has to be one of the best. You can hardly tell it's not the regular spaghetti you grew up on!

Black Bean Spaghetti

2 T olive oil
1 large onion, chopped
1 green pepper, minced
1 red pepper, chopped
6 cloves garlic, minced
4 cups cooked black beans (or 2 cans)
1 28-oz can tomato puree
½ cup chopped olives
1 tsp dried basil
¼ tsp crushed red pepper flakes
Salt and pepper to taste
1 package quinoa spaghetti
(or linguine)
1 cup fresh grated parmesan (optional)

DIRECTIONS:

1. Heat olive oil over medium heat. Add onion, green pepper and red pepper. Cook for 10 minutes, or until tender. Add garlic and cook 30 seconds. Add beans, tomato puree, olives, basil, and red pepper flakes. Salt and pepper to taste. Bring to a boil and reduce heat to a simmer. Simmer uncovered for 20 minutes.

2. Cook spaghetti according to package directions and drain. Place spaghetti on a serving platter and top with bean mixture. Top with parmesan cheese.

Make it Vegan: Either use vegan cheese or skip the cheese altogether and top with toasted pine nuts.

Make it Quick: Use a frozen pre-chopped onion and pepper medley, pre-minced garlic and chopped olives.

8 servings
Serving Size 235 g Calories 348 Total Fat 9.6g Saturated Fat 2.9g Cholesterol 11mg Sodium 299mg Total Carbohydrates 52.0g Dietary Fiber 9.3g Sugars 7.4g Protein 16.2g

I love garlic fries, but these days I do make an effort to avoid fried food when I can. These garlic polenta fries provide the flavor of garlic fries without all of the guilt! I like to serve them with my own healthy version of "aioli," which skips the mayonnaise and instead uses nonfat Greek yogurt.

Garlic Polenta Fries

2 tubes of quinoa polenta
½ cup Pecorino Romano cheese
8 cloves garlic, minced
1 T fresh parsley, minced
½ tsp sea salt
¼ tsp ground pepper
3 T olive oil, divided
Mock Garlic Aioli
1 cup nonfat Greek yogurt (I like Fage
because it is very thick)
½ tsp Dijon mustard
1 T chopped cilantro
1 tsp smoked paprika
2 T lemon juice
6 cloves garlic, minced
½ tsp mineral sea salt

DIRECTIONS:

1. Preheat oven to 450 degrees. Cut each tube of polenta into half and then cut into wedges.

2. In a small bowl, combine cheese, garlic, parsley, salt and pepper with 2 tablespoons of the olive oil. Toss carefully with polenta.

3. Spread remaining olive oil over a rimmed baking sheet. Add polenta strips in a single layer.

4. Bake, stirring at least once, for 50 minutes.

Mock Garlic Aioli

1. Combine all ingredients in a bowl until well blended. Serve as a dip or on sandwiches and burgers in place of mayonnaise.

Make it Vegan: Skip the cheese in the fries or use vegan cheese. Use light vegenaise in place of the Greek yogurt.

Make it Cleaner: Use ¼ cup cheese in fries and reduce olive oil to 2 tablespoons.

6 Servings
Calorie Content *Polenta Fries* Serving Size 201 g Amount Per Serving Calories 273 Total Fat 11.9g Saturated Fat 4.2g Trans Fat 0.0g Cholesterol 20mg Sodium 834mg Total Carbohydrates 28.8g Dietary Fiber 1.8g Protein 9.7g Calories *Mock Aioli* Serving Size 50 g Amount Per Serving Calories 32 Total Fat 0.9g Saturated Fat 0.6g Trans Fat 0.0g Cholesterol 2mg Sodium 18mg Total Carbohydrates 3.2g Sugars 1.7g Protein 3.5g

The first time I made this the results were more than a little disappointing. I used parmesan cheese and the result was a sauce that was not quite the consistency that I was looking for. I decided to tweak it and used a lighter version of the sauce I use for my macaroni and cheese, and the results were fantastic! For an extra kick, try drizzling with a little balsamic reduction.

Pasta Primavera

DIRECTIONS:

1. Cook spaghetti according to package directions. Make sure you don't undercook, and test the pasta before you drain! (Nothing worse than crunchy spaghetti!)

2. In a shallow pie plate, toast pine nuts for 5 minutes, stirring once. Set aside.

3. Bring water to boil in a large Dutch oven. Add broccoli, zucchini and carrots. Cook for 90 seconds and drain. Plunge vegetables into cold water to stop cooking and drain.

4. In a small bowl, whisk together Greek yogurt and milk.

5. Heat olive oil in a large pot. Add onion and sauté 8 minutes, or until tender. Add garlic and cook for 30 seconds. Add 1 T of olive oil and 1 T quinoa flour. Stir until well combined. Add in 1 cup of cheese and yogurt mixture. Stir until cheese melts.

6. Add in broccoli mixture, green onions, cherry tomatoes, parsley, basil, salt and pepper. Add spaghetti and toss until well coated. Sprinkle with pine nuts and remaining cheese.

1 package quinoa pasta of your choice
½ cup pine nuts
2 cups fresh broccoli
2 carrots, peeled and cut diagonally
1 zucchini, cut
⅛ cup olive oil
½ red onion, chopped fine
4 cloves of garlic, minced
1 ½ cups grated cheddar cheese
½ cup nonfat Greek yogurt
½ cup milk
1 T olive oil
1 T quinoa flour
1 cup green onions, sliced
12 cherry tomatoes, cut in half
¼ cup chopped fresh parsley
¼ cup chopped fresh basil
Salt and pepper to taste

Make it Vegan: I have to confess that I haven't tried making this dish vegan, because I'm pretty sure my kids would revolt if I tried to make them eat this many vegetables without some sort of cheese. You could, of course, use vegan cheese but ensure that you choose a brand that melts well. Otherwise I would either suggest using balsamic dressing and turning this into a fabulous pasta salad, or using cashew cream for a creamy alternative.

Make it Gluten-Free: Most quinoa pasta and flour is gluten-free, but not all! Make sure you check the label!

Make it Quick: Buy a medley of pre-cut vegetables and use jarred minced garlic.

8 servings
Calories 371 Total Fat 19.4g Saturated Fat 5.9g Trans Fat 0.0g Cholesterol 24mg Sodium 179mg Total Carbohydrates 39.5g Dietary Fiber 6.4g Sugars 8.7g Protein 13.7g

When I was growing up and in my 20s, lasagna was one of my favorite foods. As I've gotten a little bit older, the heaviness of traditional lasagna has become a bit much for me. This version gives me all of the flavors without leaving me feeling heavy. I've used kale here, but spinach would work beautifully as well—choose whichever you prefer or have on hand.

Polenta Lasagna

Sauce
1 T olive oil
1 medium onion, diced fine
2 tsp minced garlic
28 oz crushed tomatoes
1 cup water
2 6-oz cans tomato paste
8 oz tomato sauce
1 tsp Italian seasoning
½ tsp crushed red pepper
1 tsp mineral sea salt
½ tsp fresh ground black pepper

Cheese Filling
15 oz low-fat ricotta cheese
4 oz goat cheese, softened
½ tsp crushed red pepper flakes

Lasagna
12 oz kale
2 18-oz packages of quinoa polenta
1 cup low-fat mozzarella cheese
½ cup freshly grated parmesan cheese

DIRECTIONS:

1. Make Sauce: Heat 1 T olive oil in a large Dutch oven over medium heat. Add onion and sauté for 8 minutes or until tender. Add garlic and cook for another 30 seconds. Add in crushed tomatoes, tomato paste, tomato sauce, water, Italian seasoning, crushed red pepper, salt and pepper. Bring to a simmer and then reduce heat to low. Simmer for 45 minutes.

2. Make Cheese Filling: Combine ricotta cheese, goat cheese and crushed red pepper flakes

3. Bring a large pot of water to a boil. Place kale in pot and boil for 3 minutes. Drain, removing as much of the liquid as possible.

4. Preheat oven to 350 degrees. Put ¾ cup of the sauce at the bottom of a large baking dish. Cut each tube of quinoa polenta into 18 pieces. Place half of polenta on top of sauce. Top with half of cheese and sprinkle with half of the kale. Cover with sauce and repeat the layers, ending in a layer of sauce. Top with mozzarella cheese and sprinkle with parmesan. Bake for 35 minutes. Allow to cool for 10 minutes prior to serving.

Make it Quick: Instead of making the sauce, just choose the jarred version that you prefer. Buy grated cheeses and this dish comes together very quickly.

Make it Cleaner: Double the amount of kale and use fat-free cheese if desired. (Personally I'm not a big fan of fat-free.)

8 servings
Serving Size 489 g Calories 441 Total Fat 16.9g Saturated Fat 9.7g Trans Fat 0.0g Cholesterol 59mg Sodium 1451mg Total Carbohydrates 47.7g Dietary Fiber 7.8g Sugars 14.7g Protein 27.7g

This recipe was inspired by a Vegetarian Times recipe, although the original was a little bland for me and I've done some tweaking. I've called for toasted walnuts here, but if you have the time, it's worth making balsamic walnuts. Just put 1 T balsamic vinegar and 3 T agave nectar or maple syrup in the microwave for a minute. Toss with ¾ cup walnuts and bake on a lined baking sheet for 10 minutes. Save the remainder in an airtight container.

Quinoa Pasta with Goat Cheese Cream Sauce

1 package quinoa pasta shells
1 cup frozen baby peas, thawed
2 tsp olive oil
6 cloves garlic, minced
1 cup prepared creamy tomato soup
¼ cup nonfat Greek yogurt
2 T milk
1 T white wine
⅛ tsp cayenne pepper
4 oz goat cheese
2 T walnuts, toasted

DIRECTIONS:

1. Cook pasta according to package directions, adding in peas the last 3 minutes of cooking.

2. Heat olive oil in a separate pot over medium heat. Sauté garlic for 30 seconds, stirring constantly. Add soup, yogurt, milk and wine. Bring to simmer over medium-high heat. Reduce to medium-low and cook for 3 more minutes.

3. Add in 3 oz of the goat cheese and cook until melted, about 3 minutes.

4. Add cayenne pepper and season to taste with salt and pepper. Toss with pasta, peas and walnuts and serve with remaining 1 oz of goat cheese sprinkled on top.

Make it Gluten-Free: Choose a gluten-free soup and double check that the quinoa pasta you've chosen is gluten-free.

Make it Cleaner: Use olive oil spray. Choose a low-fat tomato soup and reduce the goat cheese by half. If you like, substitute broth for the wine.

Make it Vegan: In place of the Greek yogurt, place ¼ cup vegan yogurt in a strainer lined with cheese cloth. Place over a bowl and cover. Allow to strain in the refrigerator for 3 hours. Use vegan cheese in place of goat cheese (I really like homemade nut cheese here).

Serves 6
Serving Size 145 g Amount Per Serving Calories 302 Total Fat 11.0g Saturated Fat 5.3g Trans Fat 0.0g Cholesterol 23mg Sodium 201mg Total Carbohydrates 39.1g Dietary Fiber 4.3g Sugars 4.5g Protein 12.6g

When my husband asked me what I was making and I told him I was making a pasta with spinach and cannellini beans, he looked at me crazy and then proceeded to ask what else we had in the refrigerator in case he didn't like it. I smiled smugly, because I know he can't resist a dish with the bite that this has from the crushed red pepper and garlic. I was right and he asked for seconds.

Quinoa Pasta with Spinach & Beans

DIRECTIONS:

1. Cook pasta according to package directions.

2. Spray pan with olive oil spray. Add sun-dried tomatoes and spinach and cook until spinach is wilted. Add cannellini beans and cook until warm.

3. In a small bowl, combine olive oil, sea salt, black pepper, crushed red pepper and garlic.

4. Combine warm cooked pasta with spinach mixture and toss with olive oil mixture. Top with parmesan cheese.

1 package corkscrew quinoa pasta
10 oz fresh baby spinach
½ cup sun-dried tomatoes, chopped
2 cups (1 can) cannellini beans (cooked)
2 T extra-virgin olive oil
1 tsp mineral sea salt
½ tsp fresh ground black pepper
¼ tsp crushed red pepper
4 cloves garlic
½ cup parmesan cheese, grated

Make it Vegan: This dish would be great with most any nut sprinkled on top instead of the cheese.

Make it Gluten-Free: Most quinoa pasta is gluten-free, but it is important to always check.

6 servings
Serving Size 197 g Amount Per Serving Calories 313 Total Fat 9.7g Saturated Fat 2.3g Trans Fat 0.0g Cholesterol 7mg Sodium 480mg Total Carbohydrates 47.0g Dietary Fiber 7.7g Sugars 1.0g Protein 11.8g

I just love polenta, but until recently I had never tried quinoa polenta. I must say, I was very pleasantly surprised at how delicious it was. I didn't tell my guests that there was quinoa in it and no one seemed to notice the difference. If you haven't tried quinoa polenta, this is a great way to test it out! It is a healthier alternative to regular polenta without sacrificing any taste. Using polenta instead of bread, this is an easy-to-make but impressive appetizer.

Quinoa Polenta Wedges with Tapenade

1 package quinoa polenta
½ cup sun-dried tomatoes
¼ cup kalamata olives
¼ cup red onion, diced fine
¼ cup feta cheese
1 T olive oil
1 T parsley
1 T capers
6 cloves garlic

DIRECTIONS:

1. Preheat broiler and prepare a cookie sheet with olive oil.

2. Combine sun-dried tomatoes, olives, red onion, feta, olive oil, parsley, capers and garlic in a food processor. Pulse until roughly chopped.

3. Cut polenta into 12 even slices and place on cookie sheet.

4. Broil for 12 minutes until slightly brown. Cover and broil another 5 minutes. (Be sure to watch carefully so it doesn't burn).

5. Cut polenta into 4 wedges and top with tapenade.

Make it Quick: If you are tight on time, purchase a pre-made tapenade. Top with feta and capers and cook.

Make it Vegan: Just skip the cheese! There is no need to add anything else as the rest of the flavors stand well on their own.

Serves 6
Serving Size 113 g Calories 128 Total Fat 4.3g Saturated Fat 1.3g Trans Fat 0.0g Cholesterol 6mg Sodium 481mg Total Carbohydrates 18.0g Dietary Fiber 1.8g Sugars 2.2g Protein 3.6g

This is a healthier twist on a dish from Southern Living. *Don't worry—it's still quite an indulgence. If you want to use whole wheat pasta and have a problem finding it, try using whole wheat lasagna noodles and rolling them.*

Roasted Red Pepper Quinoa Cannelloni

8 oz whole wheat manicotti or cannelloni shells
1 ½ cups cooked quinoa
2 cups frozen chopped spinach, thawed
1 8-oz chive and onion cream cheese, softened
1 8-oz low-fat cream cheese, softened
8 oz part-skim mozzarella
1 tsp garlic salt
½ tsp black pepper
½ tsp red pepper flakes
Roasted Red Pepper Sauce
1 10-oz jar of roasted red peppers, diced
2 T minced garlic
1 T basil
1 ½ cups nonfat Greek yogurt
1 cup low-fat milk
½ cup parmesan cheese
Salt and pepper to taste

DIRECTIONS:

1. Preheat oven to 350 degrees. Cook pasta according to package directions.

2. Meanwhile, combine quinoa, spinach, cream cheese, mozzarella, salt, pepper and pepper flakes in a large bowl.

3. When pasta is done, allow to cool to handle. Using kitchen shears, cut pasta lengthwise. Spoon quinoa/cheese mixture into pasta and place, cut-side down, in a prepared baking dish.

4. Top with red pepper sauce and bake for 25 minutes.

Roasted Red Pepper Sauce

1. Place red peppers, garlic and basil in a medium saucepan over medium heat. Cook for 10 minutes. Allow to cool slightly and then puree in a food processor. Return to heat and bring to a boil.

2. In a small bowl, combine yogurt and milk with a whisk. Add to pepper mixture, along with parmesan cheese, salt and pepper. Reduce heat to a simmer and cook for 5 minutes.

Make it Quick: If you are pressed for time, skip the red pepper sauce and used tomato-basil marinara. Or you can combine a jar of roasted red peppers with a jar of alfredo (low-fat preferred) and that parmesan cheese as the original recipe did.

Make it Vegan: Use vegan cheese and vegan cream cheese (such as Follow Your Heart Vegan Gourmet Cream Cheese or Tofutti Better than Cream Cheese). In the sauce, use your favorite dairy-free milk in place of the cow's milk, vegan plain yogurt and vegan cheese. If you have the time, use cashew cream in place of the milk and yogurt. To make it, soak 2 cups of raw cashews overnight. Rinse and place in a blender with water to cover. Process until very fine. It will take a powerful 1000-watt blender to get cashews smooth. If yours doesn't do the job, simply strain off any lumpy pieces with the same colander that you use for washing quinoa.

Make it Cleaner: Use nonfat cheeses and reduce the cream cheese by a third.

Make it Gluten-Free: Use the gluten-free pasta of your choice. If you can't find cannelloni or manicotti shells, use lasagna noodles.

Serves 8
Serving Size 249 g Calories 367 Total Fat 12.8g Saturated Fat 7.2g Trans Fat 0.0g Cholesterol 49mg Sodium 708mg Total Carbohydrates 34.6g Dietary Fiber 4.4g Sugars 7.1g Protein 27.4g

My family loves pizza, but even I was skeptical that I could make a good pizza dough with quinoa flour. It just smells a little . . . . funny. I knew I'd succeeded when my Mom, not knowing I'd used quinoa flour, said it was the best pizza crust I've ever made. I tried to use whole wheat flour, but even my pizza-loving little guy who typically loves whole wheat wouldn't touch it. Whole wheat white flour did work nicely, however. You'll need to start the crust a day ahead!

Roasted Red Pepper, Olive & Three Cheese Pizza

DIRECTIONS:

1. Remove pizza dough from refrigerator. Sprinkle flour on clean countertops. Form a ball and allow to rest for 45 minutes.

2. Place pizza stone on the bottom rack of the oven. Preheat oven to 500 degrees and allow stone to heat for at least 30 minutes.

3. Sprinkle ground flax seeds on counter, if using. Press dough into a cake form. Using more flour as needed, stretch dough with your hands or a rolling pin. The dough should form a large pizza.

4. Transfer dough to a pizza peel or the back of a baking sheet coated with flour. Combine minced garlic, olive oil and crushed red pepper. Brush onto pizza dough.

5. Spread ricotta cheese. Top with crumbled goat cheese, olives and red pepper. Sprinkle with parmesan cheese and dried oregano.

6. Quickly transfer to pizza stone. Bake at 500 degrees for 10 minutes or until golden.

Quinoa Pizza Crust

1. In the bowl of a stand mixer, combine flours, sugar, honey, salt, yeast and olive oil. Add 1 ¼ cups of cool water and with the paddle attachment mix at low speed for a minute or two until dough comes together in a coarse ball. Add more water or flour as needed for dough to come together. Allow to rest for 5 minutes.

2. Switch to dough hook. Knead dough for 3 minutes, adding water or flour as needed to produce a ball that is smooth and not sticky. (It should be a little tacky.) You can also knead by hand.

3. Lightly oil a bowl that is twice the size of the dough. Roll dough to coat with oil. Cover with plastic wrap and chill for at least 8 hours and up to 3 days.

4. Dough should make 2 large pizzas or 4 individual pizzas. You may freeze the dough after kneading in zip top freezer bags. Thaw in the refrigerator overnight prior to using.

½ recipe Quinoa Pizza Crust
1 T olive oil
3 cloves garlic, minced
¼ tsp crushed red pepper (more to taste)
½ cup low-fat ricotta cheese
2 oz goat cheese
½ cup kalamata olives, sliced
1 roasted red pepper, drained and diced
¼ cup fresh grated parmesan cheese
1 tsp dried oregano
Ground flax seeds (optional)
Quinoa Pizza Crust
(Adapted from *Fine Cooking*)
1 ¾ cups unbleached flour (for gluten-free alternative use brown rice flour)
1 ¾ cups quinoa flour
2 tsp honey
2 ½ tsp mineral sea salt
1 package pizza-dough yeast
1 ½ T extra-virgin olive oil

> **Make it Quick:** The pizza dough can be made ahead and frozen, or kept in the refrigerator for up to 3 days. This makes it perfect for those days when you are trying to get dinner on the table, but have other things to do. Just take the dough out of the refrigerator and let it rest when you get home, and then when it's time to make dinner you can be done in no time!

Serves 6
Serving Size 108 g Calories 304 Total Fat 13.8g Saturated Fat 4.7g Trans Fat 0.0g Cholesterol 20mg Sodium 1056mg Total Carbohydrates 33.2g Dietary Fiber 2.7g Sugars 4.0g Protein 11.8g

Like the pizza crust recipe, this is an adaptation from Fine Cooking. I wasn't going to include it, but it is such a family favorite that I just couldn't resist sharing.

Sun-Dried Tomato & Goat Cheese Pizza

½ recipe Quinoa Pizza Crust
25 cloves roasted garlic
2 T olive oil, divided
2 cloves garlic, minced
10 sun-dried tomatoes, chopped
6 oz goat cheese
2 T capers
Oregano
Quinoa Pizza Crust
(Adapted from *Fine Cooking*)
1 ¾ cups unbleached flour (for gluten-free alternative use brown rice flour)
1 ¾ cups quinoa flour
2 tsp honey
2 ½ tsp mineral sea salt
1 package pizza-dough yeast
1 ½ T extra-virgin olive oil

DIRECTIONS:

1. Remove pizza dough from refrigerator. Sprinkle flour on clean countertops. Form a ball and allow to rest for 45 minutes. While dough is resting, mix garlic with 1 T olive oil. Place in a pan and cover with foil. Cook for 35 minutes at 350 degrees.

2. Place pizza stone on the bottom rack of the oven. Preheat oven to 500 degrees and allow stone to heat for at least 30 minutes.

3. Sprinkle ground flax seeds on counter, if using. Press dough into a cake form. Using more flour as needed, stretch dough with your hands or a rolling pin. The dough should form a large pizza.

4. Transfer dough to a pizza peel or the back of a baking sheet coated with flour. Combine minced garlic, olive oil and crushed red pepper. Brush onto pizza dough.

5. Spread roasted garlic on crust. Top with sun-dried tomatoes, goat cheese, capers and oregano.

6. Bake at 500 degrees for 10 minutes or until golden.

Quinoa Pizza Crust

1. In the bowl of a stand mixer, combine flours, sugar, honey, salt, yeast and olive oil. Add 1 ¼ cups of cool water and with the paddle attachment mix at low speed for a minute or two until dough comes together in a coarse ball. Add more water or flour as needed for dough to come together. Allow to rest for 5 minutes.

2. Switch to dough hook. Knead dough for 3 minutes, adding water or flour as needed to produce a ball that is smooth and not sticky. (It should be a little tacky.) You can also knead by hand.

3. Lightly oil a bowl that is twice the size of the dough. Roll dough to coat with oil. Cover with plastic wrap and chill for at least 8 hours and up to 3 days.

4. Dough should make 2 large pizzas or 4 individual pizzas. You may freeze the dough after kneading in zip top freezer bags. Thaw in the refrigerator overnight prior to using.

Make it Quick: The pizza dough can be made ahead and frozen or kept in the refrigerator for up to 3 days. This makes it perfect for those days when you are trying to get dinner on the table, but have other things to do. Just take the dough out of the refrigerator and let it rest when you get home, and then when it's time to make dinner you can be done in no time!

Serves 6
Serving Size 101 g Amount Per Serving Calories 383 Total Fat 20.2g Saturated Fat 8.2g Trans Fat 0.0g Cholesterol 30mg Sodium 982mg Total Carbohydrates 36.1g Dietary Fiber 2.7g Sugars 3.3g Protein 14.5g

Breads & Muffins

This was one of my first attempts at baking with quinoa flour. My youngest son—who is 5—is a lot like me in that he could live on carbohydrates. Unfortunately, for him that means pasta and pizza. Any time I can get quinoa (even quinoa flour!) in him I feel like I'm doing a good job. This healthier muffin is considered a treat around our house! Feel free to use agave nectar (⅓ cup) and reduce the milk by 2 tablespoons.

Blueberry Muffins

DIRECTIONS:

1. Preheat oven to 375 degrees. Beat together sugar and butter.

2. In a separate bowl, beat egg and then add in milk.

3. Sift together dry ingredients and add alternating milk and egg mixture with sugar mixture.

4. With a spoon, fold in floured blueberries. Pour into greased muffin tins and bake for 25 to 30 minutes.

½ cup sugar

⅓ cup butter, softened

1 egg

½ cup low-fat milk

¾ cup unbleached white flour

¾ cup quinoa flour

2 tsp baking powder

½ tsp salt

¼ tsp baking soda

1 ½ cup blueberries, dredged in 3 T quinoa flour

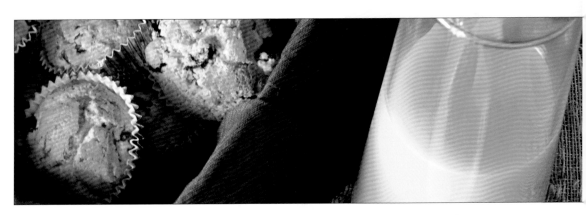

12 servings
Calories 169 Total Fat 6.4g Saturated Fat 3.4g Trans Fat 0.0g Cholesterol 30mg Sodium 174mg Total Carbohydrates 25.3g Dietary Fiber 1.9g Sugars 10.8g

This is an adaptation of the banana bread recipe on the website. Here, I've skipped the sugar and instead used agave nectar. I've also cut the butter in half and used applesauce in its place. The result is a moist banana bread that my family devoured.

Healthy Banana Bread

DIRECTIONS:

1. Preheat oven to 350 degrees.

2. In a large mixing bowl, combine agave nectar, butter and applesauce.

3. Blend in eggs, one at a time.

4. Add vanilla and mix well.

5. In a separate bowl, combine flours, baking soda and salt. Add to the mixing bowl and blend completely.

6. Add in Greek yogurt, walnuts and bananas and blend until smooth.

7. Spray a 9×5 loaf pan and place mixture in pan.

8. Bake at 350 for 1 hour. You know it is done when a toothpick comes out clean. Allow to cool for 15 minutes and then place on a wire rack to finish cooling. (That is, unless your family is already begging you to cut it.)

¼ cup butter, melted

¼ cup unsweetened applesauce

⅔ cup agave nectar

2 eggs

1 tsp vanilla extract

1 cup all-purpose flour

½ cup quinoa flour

1 tsp baking soda

½ tsp salt

½ cup nonfat Greek yogurt

½ cup walnuts, chopped (optional)

2 medium bananas, mashed

12 servings
Calories 202 Calories from Fat 76 Total Fat 8.5g Saturated Fat 2.9g Trans Fat 0.0g Cholesterol 42mg Sodium 245mg Total Carbohydrates 26.4g Dietary Fiber 2.9g Sugars 8.4g Protein 5.9g

My parents instantly declared these muffins the "best ever" and proceeded to thaw collard greens from the freezer to create a meal of pure Southern comfort food. I have to say, I enjoyed them myself as well! The corn is what really makes these spectacular, so make sure you don't skip it! If it is in season, steamed fresh corn would be really spectacular. These muffins freeze well.

Jalapeño Red Pepper Corn Muffins

DIRECTIONS:

1. Prepare a muffin tin with olive oil spray. Preheat oven to 400 degrees.

2. Sift flours, salt and baking powder together. Stir in cornmeal and brown sugar.

3. In a small bowl, beat egg, walnut oil and buttermilk. Add to dry ingredients and stir until just combined. Be careful not to overmix.

4. Stir in jalapeños, red pepper, basil and corn.

5. Spoon into muffin cups and bake for 25 minutes. Cool for 5 minutes and then turn out onto a wire rack.

½ cup rice flour (or all-purpose)
½ cup quinoa flour
½ tsp mineral sea salt
4 tsp baking powder
1 cup yellow cornmeal
1 T brown sugar
1 egg
¼ cup walnut oil
⅔ cup low-fat buttermilk
2 T jarred minced jalapeños (more or less, to taste)
1 red pepper, diced small
2 T fresh basil, chopped
2 cups frozen corn, thawed (or fresh)

12 servings
Calories 140 3.1g Trans Fat 0.0g Cholesterol 16mg Sodium 158mg Total Carbohydrates 24.9g Dietary Fiber 2.4g Sugars 3.0g Protein 4.4g

This is the perfect dish to take to your next book club or girls get-together! I seriously had to stop myself from eating with this one. It's the perfect comfort food!

Quinoa Biscuit Scroll

DIRECTIONS:

1. Preheat oven to 400 degrees. Make filling by combining cheddar, parmesan, onion, quinoa, red pepper and parsley. Salt and pepper to taste.

2. Sift flours, baking powder and salt together. Cut in butter until crumbly. Make a well in the center and add buttermilk. Mix until well combined.

3. Knead dough by hand or in a stand mixer with a bread hook until smooth and elastic.

4. Roll into a 20 x 10 rectangle. Sprinkle filling on top, leaving a 1 inch border. Roll dough up lengthwise. Bring ends together to form a ring, brushing with water to seal.

5. Place on parchment paper on a baking sheet. Cut edges with kitchen shears at regular intervals. Bake for 15 minutes. Reduce heat to 350 and bake for 20 more minutes.

6. Brush with olive oil and allow to cool.

1 cup cheddar, shredded
½ cup parmesan, shredded
1 onion, diced small
1 cup cooked quinoa
1 red pepper, diced
¼ cup diced fresh parsley
2 cups self-rising flour
1 cup quinoa flour
½ tsp baking powder
2 tsp mineral sea salt
¼ cup cubed butter
1 ¼ cups buttermilk
2 T olive oil

12 servings
Serving Size 113 g Calories 275 Total Fat 9.9g Saturated Fat 4.1g Trans Fat 0.0g Cholesterol 17mg Sodium 414mg Total Carbohydrates 35.3g Dietary Fiber 2.6g Sugars 2.5g Protein 10.4g

This is a great alternative to pita chips for dipping with hummus, and would also be great alongside most any meal. My boys liked them too, and I had to stop them from eating them all before I could get a picture taken! That means it was a winner at my house!

Quinoa Grissini

DIRECTIONS:

1. In a small bowl, mix yeast, honey and ½ cup warm water. Cover and let sit for 10 minutes.

2. Heat honey, milk and butter in a small saucepan until butter is melted.

3. Mix 2 cups quinoa flour and 1 ½ cups all-purpose flour with salt. Pour in yeast and milk mixture. Add remaining flour as needed to form a smooth dough. Knead with the bread hook in a stand mixer for 10 minutes.

4. Divide dough into 16 pieces and roll out into pencil-like strips. Place on prepared baking sheet. Cover and allow to sit for 20 minutes. Preheat oven to 425.

5. Brush with water and top with sesame seeds and poppy seeds as desired. (Sea salt works great, too!) Bake for 15 minutes.

6. Remove from oven and allow to cool on wire rack. Reduce oven temperature to 350 degrees. Bake for an additional 5 minutes, until crisp.

1 envelope active dry yeast
1 T honey
²/₃ cup milk
3 T butter
2 cups all-purpose flour
2 cups quinoa flour
1 ½ tsp mineral sea salt
Sesame seeds and poppy seeds

12 servings
Serving Size 64 g Amount Per Serving Calories 203 Total Fat 4.7g Saturated Fat 2.0g Trans Fat 0.0g Cholesterol 9mg Sodium 263mg Total Carbohydrates 33.5g Dietary Fiber 2.1g Sugars 2.9g Protein 5.5g

Desserts

If you are looking for something to satisfy your chocolate craving without completely blowing your diet, this is the dish for you. The almond extract really adds a special touch, which means you won't miss all the extra fat that is normally in chocolate desserts. This recipe is adapted from Cooking Light.

Almond Fudge Quinoa Brownies

½ cup all-purpose flour
½ cup quinoa flour
½ cup unsweetened cocoa
¼ tsp salt
⅓ cup butter
¼ cup chocolate chips
⅔ cup agave nectar
¼ cup low-fat milk
1 tsp almond extract
1 egg
2 egg yolks
½ cup slivered almonds

DIRECTIONS:

1. Preheat oven to 350 degrees.

2. Combine dry ingredients in a large bowl.

3. Put chocolate chips and butter in a bowl and heat on high in the microwave for 45 seconds, stirring every 15 seconds. Allow to cool slightly.

4. Combine agave nectar, milk, vanilla, almond extract, egg yolks and egg with butter mixture and whisk until well combined. Add dry ingredients and stir until just combined. Stir in almonds.

5. Pour batter in an 8-inch square metal pan that has been well sprayed with olive oil spray. Bake for 20 minutes.

12 servings
Calories 174 Total Fat 10.2g Saturated Fat 4.8g Trans Fat 0.0g Cholesterol 65mg Sodium 100mg Total Carbohydrates 18.5g Dietary Fiber 2.6g Sugars 7.6g

Cookies are one of the hardest things to make lighter, because it is so difficult to replicate the texture of white sugar, butter and eggs. Here, we skip the white sugar completely and add in quinoa flakes and flour for an extra punch of protein. I've included gluten-free substitutions below. Make this healthier by using dark chocolate.

Chocolate Cherry Chip Quinoa Cookies

DIRECTIONS:

1. Preheat oven to 350 degrees.

2. Measure dry ingredients using a knife to level measuring cups. Combine ingredients through salt in a large mixing bowl.

3. Heat a saucepan over medium heat and melt butter. Remove from heat and mix in brown sugar.

4. Add sugar and butter to flour mixture and beat over high heat until well combined. Add cherries, vanilla and egg and beat until combined. Stir in chocolate chips.

5. Prepare cookie sheet with olive oil spray. Drop cookies by the spoonful. Bake for 10–12 minutes.

$^1/_3$ cup whole wheat white flour (substituted brown rice flour for gluten-free)
$^1/_3$ cup quinoa flour
1 cup quinoa flakes
½ cup old-fashioned oatmeal (gluten-free or just use quinoa flakes)
1 tsp baking soda
¾ tsp mineral sea salt
6 T unsalted butter
¾ cup light brown sugar, packed
1 cup tart dried cherries
1 tsp vanilla
1 egg, beaten
½ cup mini chocolate chips

Calories 120 Total Fat 4.6g Saturated Fat 2.6g Trans Fat 0.0g Cholesterol 16mg Sodium 139mg Total Carbohydrates 17.7g Dietary Fiber 2.2g Sugars 8.9g Protein 1.9g

*What could be better than a dessert that is so easy you can make it in your crock pot?
This is healthy and delicious!*

Crock Pot Pear & Blueberry Crumble

DIRECTIONS:

2/3 cup old-fashioned oats
2/3 cup quinoa flakes
1/2 cup quinoa flour
1/2 tsp baking powder
1/4 tsp mineral sea salt
3 T olive oil
3 T cold butter
3 T agave nectar
6 pears, peeled and sliced
1 cup blueberries
1/3 cup agave nectar
Juice of 1 lemon
1/2 cup pomegranate juice

1. Preheat oven to 350 degrees. In the bowl of a food processer, combine oats, quinoa flakes, quinoa flour, baking powder and sea salt. Pulse to combine. Add in olive oil, butter and agave nectar and process until well combined. Place in a single layer on a baking sheet. Bake for 10 minutes. Stir. Bake for an additional 5 to 8 minutes or until lightly golden brown.

2. Combine sliced pears and blueberries in a bowl. Toss with agave nectar and lemon juice. Spray crock pot with olive oil spray.

3. Place a layer of the crumble on the bottom. Top with half of the pears and blueberries and follow with another layer of crumble. Repeat layering, finishing with a layer of crumble. Pour pomegranate juice on top and cook on low for 4 to 6 hours.

8 servings
Calories 299 Total Fat 11.0g Saturated Fat 3.5g Trans Fat 0.0g Cholesterol 11mg Sodium 97mg Total Carbohydrates 48.1g Dietary Fiber 7.8g Sugars 25.9g Protein 3.5g

When I heard they were making a new chocolate bar with quinoa and I couldn't find it in the store, I decided to make my own. Rather than baking the quinoa, which yields a very firm texture, I've popped it here. The method is just like popping popcorn, but don't expect the quinoa to get big like a popcorn kernel does! The change in appearance is subtle, but the change in texture is fairly significant. Unless you are watching your sodium, don't skip the salt here. It sounds counterintuitive but does wonders for the taste! If you are new to working with chocolate, one thing that you must remember is that chocolate and water are enemies. A single drop is enough to destroy all of your hard work and render smooth chocolate a mess. Here I've paired the Almond Bark with coffee ice cream for a special treat, but I can assure you that it works well on its own as well.

Quinoa Chocolate Bark Sundae

DIRECTIONS:

½ cup quinoa, rinsed and dried
1 T olive oil
1 lb dark or bittersweet chocolate, chopped and divided
1 cup almonds, toasted and chopped
1 tsp sea salt
Coffee ice cream and whipped cream (optional)

1. After rinsing your quinoa, spread it out on a cookie sheet to dry. Alternatively, cook over low in a skillet until dry. Place olive oil in a popcorn popper and allow to get warm. Add quinoa and cook about 5 minutes, until quinoa is lightly brown. Alternatively, pop the quinoa in a covered saucepan, shaking to prevent burning.

2. Line a baking sheet with parchment paper

3. Place chocolate in a microwave and heat for 40 seconds. Stir and cook in 30 second increments until melted.

4. In a small bowl, combine popped quinoa, almonds and sea salt. Add ¾ of mixture to the melted chocolate and pour onto parchment paper. Top with remaining quinoa mixture.

5. Allow to sit until firm, about 2 hours. Break into pieces. If desired, serve with coffee ice cream and whipped cream.

18 servings
Serving Size 36 g Amount Per Serving Calories 171 Total Fat 10.3g Saturated Fat 4.5g Trans Fat 0.0g Cholesterol 0mg Sodium 106mg Total Carbohydrates 20.8g Dietary Fiber 0.9g Sugars 13.7g Protein 3.4g

I use the term crumb cake very loosely here. The recipe is very loosely based on a recipe from Cooks Illustrated. *A crumb cake was what I originally intended, but thanks to using agave nectar my crumbs weren't very crumbly. When I put this in the oven I was convinced that it was a cooking disaster, but surprisingly this was one of the family favorites. My Dad even snuck some off in the freezer for himself. These are more like a cookie-cake but the flavor is fantastic!*

Raspberry Crumb Cake

DIRECTIONS:

1. To make topping, whisk together ½ cup all-purpose flour, ¼ cup quinoa flour, brown sugar and ½ tsp mineral sea salt. Add in applesauce, melted butter, 1 ½ T agave nectar and water and mix until small pieces form. Add ½ cup of almond paste and combine. Set aside.

2. Heat oven to 350 degrees. Spray a 13 x 9 pan with olive oil spray.

3. Combine remaining ¾ cup all-purpose flour and ½ cup quinoa flour with baking powder and ½ tsp salt.

4. In a small bowl, whisk together yogurt, eggs, vanilla and almond extracts.

5. Use an electric mixer on medium-high speed and beat together remaining 2 ½ T agave nectar, ¾ stick softened butter, and remaining almond paste for 2 minutes. Add yogurt mixture and combine well. Add in flour mixture on low speed and combine well. Once ingredients are well combined, beat on high for 1 minute.

6. Spread filling in prepared pan. Carefully spread jam and cover with topping. Bake for 40 to 50 minutes until firm.

Filling
12 oz raspberry jam (or jam of your choice)
Cake
1 ¼ cup all-purpose flour
¾ cup quinoa flour
4 T agave nectar
¼ cup light brown sugar
1 tsp mineral sea salt
2 T unsweetened applesauce
2 T unsalted butter, melted, plus ¾ stick
1 T water
7 oz almond paste, crumbled into small pieces
1 ½ tsp baking powder
1/3 cup Greek nonfat yogurt
2 large eggs
1 tsp vanilla extract
1 tsp almond extract

16 servings
Serving Size 76 g Calories 268 Total Fat 10.3g Saturated Fat 4.2g Trans Fat 0.0g Cholesterol 42mg Sodium 171mg Total Carbohydrates 40.6g Dietary Fiber 1.4g Sugars 21.6g Protein 4.4g

Quinoa for Kids

Over the summer, my husband got in the habit of taking my boys to get miniature donuts at a popular chain. One day they came home with four still in their packaging. I happened to glance at the ingredient list and was shocked at how long it was and how many ingredients failed to pass the "Could a third grader say the word?" rule. So, I immediately ordered a miniature cake donut pan and set out to create my own recipe. These were a hit at our house!

Cake Donuts

DIRECTIONS:

1. Preheat oven to 350 degrees.

2. Measure out a cup of whole wheat white flour. Remove 2 tablespoons of the flour and return to the flour bin. Place flour in a sifter and add two tablespoons of cornstarch, 2 teaspoons baking powder, 1 teaspoon salt, coconut palm sugar and cinnamon. Sift.

3. Place melted butter, eggs, quinoa, buttermilk and vanilla in a blender or food processor. Process until smooth.
Pour wet ingredients into dry ingredients and mix until just combined.

4. Place batter (it will be thick) in a miniature cake donut pan about ⅔ of the way full. Bake for 8 to 10 minutes, until a toothpick comes out clean. (If you are using a full-size donut pan you will need to adjust cooking time accordingly.)

5. Remove from oven and take a butter knife and run it around the edges of the donuts. Allow to cool in the pan for 5 to 10 minutes and remove from pan, using the butter knife again on the ones that do not easily pop out. Allow to completely cool on a wire rack.

6. Top with glaze or sugar. To make sugar donuts, place evaporated cane sugar (or other sugar of choice) in a plastic bag and add 2 to 3 cooled donuts at a time. Shake until coated. To make a glaze, combine ¼ cup water and a teaspoon of vanilla in a small saucepan. Heat until warm and add 2 cups of confectioners' sugar. Stir with a whisk until smooth. Dip donuts and top with sprinkles, if desired. Allow to sit on a wire rack or parchment paper for 10 minutes prior to serving.

1 cup whole wheat white flour (or gluten-free baking mix), minus 2 T
½ cup quinoa flour
2 T cornstarch
2 tsp baking powder
1 tsp salt
¾ cup coconut palm sugar
¼ tsp cinnamon
1 T butter, melted and cooled slightly
2 eggs
1 cup quinoa
1 cup buttermilk
1 tsp vanilla

Makes 24 miniature donuts
Serving size 1 donut (not including topping) Calories 61 Total Fat 1.3g Saturated Fat .5g Trans Fat 0.0g Cholesterol 17mg Sodium 117mg Total Carbohydrates 10.3g Protein 2g

Although I do not eat meat, my boys still do. Of course, just like every other mom, I like to make sure that it is as healthy as possible! This meatloaf is easy to put together and kids love it!

Cheeseburger Meatloaf

DIRECTIONS:

1. Heat oven to 350 degrees. Spray a metal pan with cooking spray.

2. In a large bowl, combine ground beef, crumbled bacon, cooked quinoa, chopped onion, chia gel, tomato sauce, salt and pepper. Form into a loaf on prepared pan.

3. Spread sauce over loaf and bake for 35 minutes. Remove from oven and preheat broiler.
Top with shredded cheddar and, if desired, tomatoes. Broil for 2 to 3 minutes.

1 ½ lbs organic ground beef
8 strips nitrate-free turkey bacon, cooked and crumbled
1 cup cooked quinoa
¼ cup chopped onion
4 T chia gel (or 1 egg)
8 oz tomato sauce
¼ tsp salt
¼ tsp pepper
Sauce
⅓ cup ketchup
2 tablespoons prepared mustard
Topping
1 cup shredded cheddar
Sliced tomatoes (optional)

8 Servings
Calories 257 fat 8g Saturated fat 2.8g Trans Fats 0g Cholesterol 89mg Sodium 641g Carbohydrates 10g Fiber 1.8g Sugars 3.7g Protein 34.4g

Just about all kids love chicken nuggets, but unfortunately the ones you buy in the store are typically not so healthy. This recipe for chicken nuggets is one that your little ones will enjoy and you will feel good about giving them! Although it seems like a lot of ingredients, the breading freezes well. I typically make a double recipe of the breading and freeze what I don't use.

Chicken Nuggets

DIRECTIONS:

1. Preheat oven to 400 degrees.

2. Cut chicken into bite sized pieces.

3. In a food processor, combine almonds, quinoa flakes, breadcrumbs, oat bran, quinoa flour, flax seeds, parmesan cheese, salt, garlic powder and thyme. Process until smooth. Transfer mixture to a shallow dish. (I typically have breadcrumbs left over which I like to freeze, so I only put a portion in the bowl I will be using to dredge the chicken.)

4. In another shallow dish, combine egg whites and milk. Dredge chicken in milk and egg white mixture. Then dredge in breadcrumb mixture.

5. Place nuggets on a wire rack on a baking sheet. Bake for 15 minutes. Turn on broiler and broil for 5 more minutes.

1 ½ lbs boneless, skinless chicken
¼ cup almonds
¼ cup quinoa flakes
2 T whole wheat breadcrumbs or gluten- free breadcrumbs
2 T oat bran
2 T quinoa flour
2 T ground flax seeds
½ cup grated parmesan
1 tsp salt
½ tsp garlic powder
1 tsp dried thyme
2 egg whites, lightly beaten
¼ cup milk

Serves 8
Calories 235 Fat 7.5g Saturated Fat 2.1g Trans Fat 0 Cholesterol 72 mg Sodium 503 mg Carbohydrates 9.6g Dietary Fiber 1.7g Sugars 1.6 g Protein 30.8g

The idea of making homemade ice cream sandwiches using yogurt and lemon juice and sugar came from the cookbook Deceptively Delicious. After making their recipe for several years, I set out to make it a bit cleaner by skipping the boxed graham crackers and making my own quinoa cookies. Although these cookies are rather plain on their own, they work nicely to counterbalance the sweetness of the filling. By using Greek yogurt and coconut palm sugar in place of white, I've made this a treat I can feel good about serving!

Ice Cream Sandwiches

DIRECTIONS:

Cookies

1. Preheat oven to 350 degrees. Line a cookie sheet with parchment paper. Place cashews on a rimmed baking sheet and cook for 18 to 20 minutes, stirring occasionally. Remove from oven and allow to cool slightly. Place in food processor and combine.

2. Sift together the quinoa flour, whole wheat white or gluten-free flour, palm sugar and sea salt. Toss with nuts and add softened butter. The mixture will be very dry. If it is too crumbly to work with, soften with a bit of water using your hands.

3. Lightly flour your counter and roll out dough. Cut into circles using a 2 ½ inch cookie cutter. If your dough sticks, roll dough out on parchment paper. Bake for 18 minutes or until golden brown. Allow to cool completely before proceeding.

Filling

1. In a large bowl, combine vanilla yogurt, coconut palm sugar, buttermilk, lemon juice and lemon zest. Cover and place in the freezer for 2 to 3 hours, stirring occasionally and scraping sides.

2. When filling is hard enough to stick to the cookies, spoon filling on one cookie and top with another. Wrap up individually in parchment or wax paper.

Cookies
1 cup raw cashews
8 T unsalted butter, room temperature
¼ cup quinoa flour
1 cup whole wheat white flour or gluten-free flour blend
½ cup coconut palm sugar
1 ½ tsp sea salt

Filling
1 cup nonfat Greek yogurt
½ cup coconut palm sugar
½ cup low-fat buttermilk
1 T lemon juice
½ tsp lemon zest

12 servings
Calories 211 Fat 13.2 g Saturated Fat 5.8 grams Trans Fat 0 g Cholesterol 21mg Sodium 262 Carbohydrates 20.7g Fiber 2.1g Sugars 6.6g Protein 5.4g

When my boys are craving a little comfort food, Macaroni and Cheese is our go-to meal. But you won't find boxes of mac and cheese in my pantry! Although it will never be the healthiest dish on our menu, I feel good about staying away from the preservatives and chemicals that are found in boxed mac and cheese.

Macaroni and Cheese

DIRECTIONS:

1. Preheat oven to 350 degrees.

2. Cook pasta according to package directions.

3. Heat olive oil in a medium saucepan. Add in flour and cook for two to three minutes, stirring frequently. Add milk and cook until thickens, about four minutes. Turn heat to low and add cheddar cheese. Cook until cheese melts, stirring occasionally. Stir in mustard, sea salt and pepper.

4. Place in a medium baking dish and top with breadcrumbs if desired. Bake for 30 to 40 minutes.

5. Allow to sit for 15 minutes prior to serving.

1 ½ tablespoons olive oil
1 ½ tablespoons white whole wheat flour
or gluten-free flour blend
1 ¼ cups low-fat milk
¾ cup cheddar cheese
2 tsp Dijon mustard
½ tsp sea salt
¼ tsp fresh ground pepper
½ cup regular or gluten-free
breadcrumbs (optional)
8 oz quinoa pasta

Serves 6
Calories 255 Fat 9.7g Saturated Fat 3.5g Trans Fat 0g Cholesterol 16mg Sodium 298g Carbohydrates 32.8g Fiber 2.6g Sugars 3.2g Protein 9.5g

I like to keep popped quinoa on hand all the time so that I can whip up easy recipes like this Mango Parfait! Feel free to play around with this recipe. Any type of fruit would work well!

Mango Parfait with Quinoa Crunch

DIRECTIONS:

¾ cup quinoa, rinsed and dried
1 T coconut oil
2 cups nonfat Greek yogurt
1 T lime juice
1 tsp honey
1 mango, peeled and diced

1. Heat coconut oil in a popcorn popper or heavy duty saucepan. Add quinoa and pop for about 5 minutes, until the seeds become golden brown. (If you are using a saucepan you will want to cover it and shake frequently to prevent burning.) Store in an airtight container for up to 2 weeks.

2. In a large bowl, combine Greek yogurt, lime juice and honey.

3. Place diced mango in the bottom of a glass and top with yogurt and popped quinoa. Continue layers until your glass is full, ending with popped quinoa.

Serves 4
Serving Size 204 g Calories 248 Total Fat 5.3g Saturated Fat 3.1g Trans Fat 0.0g Cholesterol 7mg Sodium 47mg Total Carbohydrates 34.3g Dietary Fiber 3.1g Sugars13.3g Protein16.5g

This may be the only recipe that I've ever made and instantly said "I bet I could sell these!" Although I am not someone with much of a sweet tooth, I have to say that I have a hard time resisting these chocolate bars. The combination of the sweetness of the chocolate and the sea salt is a real winner in my book. To make these into bars, you will need a candy bar mold, which you can pick up for less than $8. If you don't want to do this, simply line a rimmed baking sheet with parchment paper.

Quinoa Chocolate Bars

DIRECTIONS:

½ cup quinoa, rinsed and dried
1 T coconut oil
1 lb chocolate cut into equal size pieces
(any type will work—white, dark, milk,
semi-sweet)
1 cup almonds, toasted and chopped
1 tsp sea salt

1. After rinsing your quinoa, spread it out on a cookie sheet to dry. Alternatively, cook over low in a skillet until dry. Place olive oil in a popcorn popper and allow to get warm. Add quinoa and cook about 5 minutes, until quinoa is lightly brown. Alternatively, pop the quinoa in a covered saucepan, shaking to prevent burning.

2. Spray candy bar molds with olive oil spray. Place chocolate in a microwave and heat for 40 seconds. Stir and cook in 30 second increments until melted, stirring in between cooking.

3. In a small bowl, combine popped quinoa, almonds and sea salt. Add ¾ of mixture to chocolate. Pour chocolate into molds and top with remaining ¼ of the popped quinoa mixture.

4. Allow to sit until firm, about 2 hours. Break into pieces. (If you just can't wait, you can also put the chocolate into the freezer for 20–45 minutes, depending on the thickness of your chocolate bars.)

Serving Size 54 g
Calories 282 Total Fat16.6g Saturated Fat 9.2g Trans Fat 0.0g Cholesterol 9mg Sodium 186mg Total Carbohydrates 28.4g Dietary Fiber 2.7g Sugars 19.8g
Protein 5.5g

This is a recipe that is made in my house at least once a week—and one I play with often. If I'm feeling a bit indulgent, I will often increase the cheese and flour to one cup and use 5 eggs instead of three. On the other hand, sometimes I skip the eggs and cheese all together and use flax seed egg replacer. Play around with this and see what works for your family. When making quinoa fritters, one thing to keep in mind is that if they are sticking to the pan the reason is typically that you are trying to flip them before they have cooked enough. Cook them a little longer and they will flip easily.

Quinoa Fritters

DIRECTIONS:

1. Heat a large saucepan to medium heat and spray with olive oil. Add quinoa and cook for 5 minutes, stirring to prevent burning. Add 1 ¼ cup of vegetable broth and bring to a simmer. Reduce to low and cover. Cook for 20 to 25 minutes. Remove from heat and allow to sit covered for five more minutes. Cool slightly.

2. In a large bowl combine cooled quinoa with flour, cheese, onion, salt, pepper and parsley. Lightly beat eggs in a small bowl and add to quinoa mixture.

3. Heat oil in a skillet over medium heat. Form quinoa into balls or ovals and carefully add to hot oil. Cook for 3–5 minutes per side, or until a golden crust has formed. Drain on paper towels.

4. For the ketchup, combine all ingredients in a small saucepan. Bring to boil over medium to medium-high heat. Reduce to medium-low and simmer for 18 minutes.

Fritters

1 cup quinoa, rinsed
1 ¼ cup vegetable broth
⅓ cup white whole wheat flour or gluten-free flour blend
⅓ cup cheddar cheese, shredded
¼ cup chopped onion
¾ tsp sea salt
¼ tsp ground black pepper
1 T chopped parsley
3 eggs
¼ cup coconut oil

Homemade Ketchup

6 oz tomato paste
¼ cup water
2 T coconut palm sugar
2 cloves garlic, minced
½ tsp sea salt
¼ tsp cumin
½ tsp dry mustard
2 T apple cider vinegar

Serving Size 127 g
Amount Per Serving (without ketchup) Calories 266 Total Fat 15.4g Saturated Fat 10.1g Cholesterol 100mg Sodium 465mg Total Carbohydrates 22.8g Dietary Fiber 2.7g Sugars 0.8g Protein 10.1g

This recipe was inspired by a recipe for pancakes in Fine Cooking that looked so delicious I had to try to make it healthier. I've used whole wheat white flour, which has all the health benefits of whole wheat flour, and of course I've added quinoa! I've also gotten rid of the white sugar and in its place used coconut palm sugar, which is low on the glycemic index. The result is without a doubt the best quinoa pancakes I've ever tried. I don't enjoy sweets in the morning and even I can't resist this recipe. The recipe also works nicely with a gluten free flour blend!

Quinoa Pancakes

DIRECTIONS:

1. If using butter, melt and set aside.

2. In a large bowl, combine whole wheat white flour, coconut palm sugar, baking powder, baking soda and sea salt. In a separate bowl, combine buttermilk, eggs, and vanilla. Add melted butter or oil to wet ingredients. Mix with dry ingredients and stir in quinoa. Let the batter rest for 5 minutes.

3. Heat skillet over medium heat. Brush with oil and pour batter onto the skillet in ¼ cup portions. Cook until bubbles rise to the surface and the edges are dry. Flip and cook for 1 more minute.

3 T melted butter, canola or coconut oil
1 ½ cups whole wheat white flour (or gluten-free flour blend)
¼ cup coconut palm sugar (or healthier sugar of your choosing)
2 ½ tsp baking powder
½ tsp baking soda
½ tsp sea salt
2 cups low-fat buttermilk
2 large eggs
1 tsp vanilla
1 cup cooked quinoa
Oil, for brushing pan

Serving Size 152 g
Amount Per Serving Calories 276 Calories from Fat 92 Total Fat 10.2g Saturated Fat 1.6g Trans Fat 0.0g Cholesterol 74mg Sodium 372mg Total Carbohydrates 36.7g Dietary Fiber1.5g Sugars 6.2g Protein 9.3g

My boys love burgers, so it is my job to make sure that the ones they eat are as healthy as possible. Here, I've snuck in not only quinoa, but oat bran and flax seeds as well. The boys have no idea they are eating a "healthier" burger. Shhh!

Sliders

DIRECTIONS:

1. In a large bowl, combine ground beef or turkey, quinoa, oat bran, flax seeds, ketchup, egg, garlic and sea salt. You will need to use your hands and almost knead the dough as you would bread. (Initially, it may seem like there is too much quinoa and oat bran, but as you knead these will work into the meat.)

2. Form into small patties. Cook on a grill, grill pan or skillet to desired doneness.

1 lb lean ground beef or turkey
1 cup cooked quinoa
½ cup oat bran
2 T ground flax seeds
¼ cup organic ketchup
1 egg, beaten
1 clove garlic, minced
½ tsp sea salt
¼ tsp black pepper

Serving Size 142 g
Amount Per Serving Calories 285 Total Fat 10.1g Saturated Fat 2.4g Cholesterol 85mg Sodium 337mg Total Carbohydrates 33.1g Dietary Fiber 5.5g
Sugars 2.7g Protein 23.3g

In our busy house, these meatballs are a lifesaver! I make them in bulk ahead of time and keep them frozen until I need them. Now I never have to panic when I hear the question, "What's for lunch, Mom?"

Spaghetti and Meatballs

DIRECTIONS:

1. Preheat oven to 500 degrees.

2. In a large bowl, combine ground beef, cooked quinoa, shredded carrots, ketchup, egg, garlic and sea salt. Form into small meatballs.

3. Place on the top of a broiler pan and bake for 12 minutes. Meanwhile, cook pasta according to package directions. Serve pasta with meatballs and marinara sauce. Top with cheese, if desired.

1 lb organic lean ground beef
1 cup cooked quinoa
$^1/_3$ cup shredded carrots
2 T ketchup
1 egg, beaten
2 cloves garlic, minced (optional)
1 tsp sea salt
8 oz quinoa pasta (or pasta of your choice)
8 oz marinara sauce

Serving Size 175 g
Amount Per Serving Calories 338 Total Fat 8.3g Saturated Fat 2.4g Trans Fat 0.0g Cholesterol 99mg Sodium 535mg Total Carbohydrates 35.5g Dietary Fiber 3.5g Sugars 3.7g Protein 28.6g

I have to give all the credit to Tosca Reno, author of the Eat-Clean Diet series, for introducing me to quinoa. The first quinoa recipe I ever tried was from her first Eat-Clean Diet book and inspired this recipe. It was love at first bite for me! This recipe is my adaptation, which succeeded in getting my then preschoolers hooked on quinoa.

Turkey Sausage Quinoa

DIRECTIONS:

1. Heat chopped turkey sausage in a medium skillet. Spray a saucepan with olive oil spray. Add onion and sun-dried tomatoes and cook for 8 minutes. Add quinoa and garlic and cook for 2 more minutes.

2. Add broth, sea salt and pepper and bring to a simmer over medium high heat. Turn to low and cover. Cook for 25 minutes. Remove from heat. Stir in parsley and sausage. Allow to sit covered for 5 more minutes. Fluff and serve.

1 cup quinoa, rinsed
½ onion, chopped fine
¼ cup sun-dried tomatoes (not packed in oil)
1 clove garlic, minced
1 ½ cup chicken or vegetable broth
½ tsp sea salt
¼ tsp fresh ground pepper
1 T parsley or cilantro, minced
8 oz nitrate-free turkey sausage, chopped small

Serves 6
Serving Size 115 g Amount Per Serving Calories 294 Calories from Fat 126 Total Fat 14.1g Saturated Fat 4.0g Trans Fat 0.1g Cholesterol 59mg Sodium 476mg
Total Carbohydrates 19.3g Dietary Fiber 2.4g Protein 21.6g

Wendy Polisi is the creator of CookingQuinoa.net, the most popular website on the Internet devoted to everything about quinoa and healthy living.

There she shares quinoa recipes and cooking tips with her more than 200,000 monthly readers, introducing them to quinoa and showing them that healthy and delicious can go hand in hand. Although she spends a great deal of time working on the website, her most important priorities are her five- and six-year-old boys whom she and her husband are homeschooling.

Wendy is an avid promoter of lifestyle design, a graduate of the University of Florida and holds a Bachelor of Science in Business Administration.

Index

My Favorite Quinoa Recipes